I Loved You Until
The ~~Morning~~
Morning

TRACEY EMIN
I LOVED YOU UNTIL THE MORNING

Martina Droth

WITH CONTRIBUTIONS BY

Claire Gilman

Courtney J. Martin

YALE CENTER FOR BRITISH ART

DISTRIBUTED BY YALE UNIVERSITY PRESS

NEW HAVEN AND LONDON

FOREWORD

The Yale Center for British Art is honored to be the first museum anywhere to present a solo exhibition of Tracey Emin's paintings. Emin established her reputation internationally in the 1990s with her seminal installation *My Bed* (1998), and her career has been defined by the innovative use of a wide variety of materials. *I Loved You Until The Morning* foregrounds Emin as a painter, her primary medium over the last two decades, and is the first museum show dedicated to this facet of her work. The exhibition highlights Emin's unique emotional language, with which she explores deeply personal experiences to confront timely issues about female sexuality and women's bodies. Her paintings lay bare intimate and private experiences that veer from the prosaic to the most profound and life-affirming aspects of being a woman. This is true in how she paints as well as what she paints. As her creative director, Harry Weller, noted in Emin's recent White Cube catalogue, she has found a way to paint that can "carry the weight of the subject." As well as paintings, the exhibition includes sculptures, a set of drawings selected by the artist from her personal archive, and a neon made especially for the occasion.

I Loved You Until The Morning inaugurates a new chapter for the YCBA, as one of two exhibitions that reopen the museum at the unveiling of its meticulous renovation. This presentation of Emin's work appears alongside an exhibition of paintings, drawings, and prints by J. M. W. Turner (1775–1851), an artist who has inspired generations of artists and with whom Emin has a uniquely personal, transhistorical relationship. In the handwritten poem addressed to him that appears as a special insert to our recent publication *Turner's Last Sketchbook*, Emin ends with the words "I Love You," a sentiment echoed in this exhibition's title. Although born nearly two hundred years apart, these artists share an understanding of the expressive potential of paint. Both served as professors at the Royal Academy of Arts in London, Turner teaching perspective and Emin, drawing, each appointment a recognition of the artist's dedication to draftsmanship as well as to teaching. Additionally, their ways of looking at the world were shaped by the seaside town of Margate, on England's east coast, where both spent formative periods of their lives. In 2017 Emin returned to Margate and in 2022 established TKE Studios and its affiliated artist residencies, providing opportunities for emerging artists and helping to revive the town's economy. Emin's commitment to arts education is longstanding, and it is fitting that this exhibition should take place in a university museum with a thriving art school.

Our heartfelt thanks go to Tracey Emin for entrusting us with this important show. Emin has been an active and generous partner in shaping the exhibition, lending paintings that are precious to her as well as producing new works that activate different spaces within our storied, Louis Kahn–designed building. A neon bearing the title of the exhibition welcomes visitors in our entrance court, and a suite of drawings displayed in our iconic Study Room contextualizes Emin within a longer history of British draftsmanship. Shown in this teaching and research space, the drawings also underscore the artist's commitment to pedagogy, which was once again in evidence during her last visit to Yale, when she led a life-drawing class at the School of Art, engaging students in hands-on practice.

There are few people who know Emin's work better than Harry Weller. His expertise encompasses everything from the conceptual development of Emin's oeuvre to the logistical complexities of installation, and we are indebted to him for his generous counsel and guidance in the planning and execution of this exhibition. Emin's galleries — White Cube, Xavier Hufkens, and Galleria Lorcan O'Neill Roma — and their dedicated staffs have provided invaluable support, connecting us with lenders and assisting with loans. We owe particular thanks to the exhibition's lenders for the generosity that enabled us to trace the evolution of Emin's paintings from 2007 to now.

While an exhibition is necessarily temporary, the legacy of this project will be long-lasting, thanks to the generous support of collections and individuals who have long championed Emin. We owe an immense debt of gratitude to the George Economou Collection for its extraordinary gift, which allows Emin's elegiac *I Followed You to the End* (2024) to join the Yale Center for British Art's collection in perpetuity. The YCBA is honored to become stewards of Emin's work, furthering our mission to judiciously expand our collection of contemporary art and enabling generations of visitors and future students at Yale to encounter her painting in person. Our sincere thanks also go to Arthur W. Zeckendorf for his generous support of our publication, which will contribute to the growing scholarship on this important artist.

The present book and exhibition would not have been possible without many dedicated supporters and colleagues. Special thanks go first and foremost to Courtney J. Martin, former director of the YCBA (2019–2024), who gave her wholehearted support to this project from the outset. It was a privilege to work with her on the development of this volume, and her illuminating interview with Emin is a fitting conclusion to the book. Our thanks also go to Claire Gilman, Acquavella Curator and Department Head, Modern and Contemporary Drawings at the Morgan Library and Museum in New York, for her insightful essay examining Emin's drawing practice. Many staff members at the YCBA and affiliates are owed a debt of gratitude for their tireless efforts in producing this book — our Head of Publications, Don McMahon, stewarded its conception and editorial shape, and our Head of Design, Julie Fry, undertook its beautiful production. In addition, thanks are owed to the book's editor, Jennifer Liese; to Sarah Resnick, an early and astute reader of the manuscript; to Rachel Stratton and Brooke Krancer for invaluable research support; and to Linda Friedlaender and Daniel Zhang, as well as Christina Ferando and Hannah Wirta Kinney, for their inspiring work on interpretation and educational programming. Many individuals at the YCBA have contributed to the coordination of the exhibition, and special thanks are owed to Charlotte Lowrey for project oversight, to Kevin Derkin and the installation team, and to Corey Myers and Mell Scalzi, registrars. In addition, Beth Miller and her team coordinated the publicity, marketing, and joyful celebration of the exhibition's opening.

I Loved You Until The Morning comes at a pivotal moment in our institutional history and in the culture at large. Tracey Emin's work has long been at the forefront in challenging gender stereotypes and bringing "taboo" subjects related to women's experience to light. These issues are in the public consciousness now more than ever. As we reopen our doors to the public, we are privileged to present the work of this fearless and groundbreaking artist.

—Martina Droth, Deputy Director and Chief Curator, Yale Center for British Art

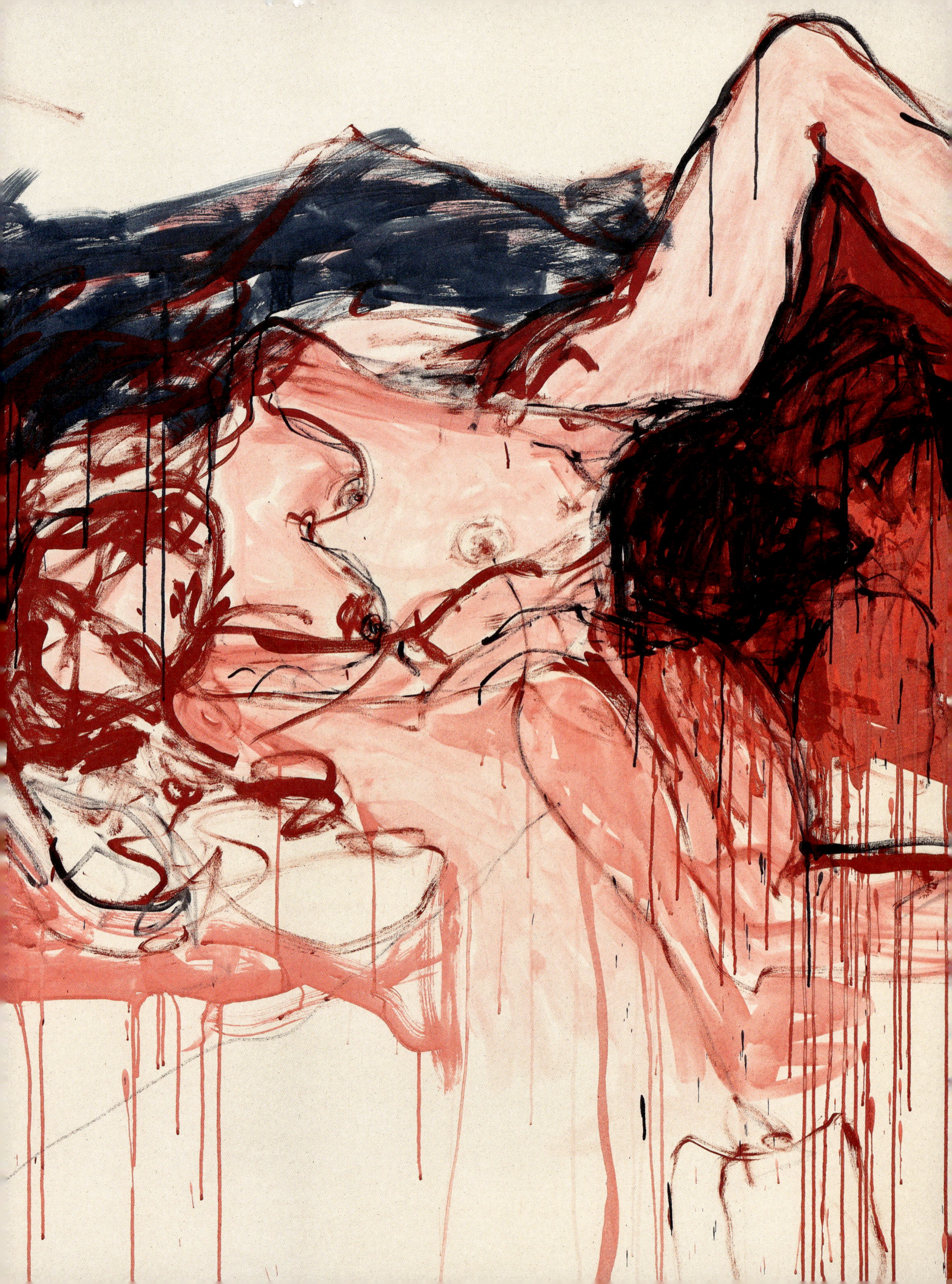

TRACEY EMIN, PAINTER

Martina Droth

With few exceptions, Tracey Emin's paintings revolve around the vast emotional consequences of ordinary life experiences. The female body is Emin's primary subject matter, sometimes rendered as a fully legible form, sometimes fragmented or partial, but she is not concerned with what the body looks like. Rather, Emin expresses the intense feelings that flow from profound yet commonplace events — pregnancy, illness, physical and psychological abuse — and how they register as palpable sensations in the body. *And It was Love* (2023; detail opposite), one of Emin's largest paintings to date, shows a naked woman from a bird's-eye view, splayed across the picture plane, the canvas doubling as a bed. A dark, undefined shape — perhaps a figure seen from above — is positioned between her open legs. Although Emin has, unusually, rendered the woman's head, the face is a schematic mask without expression. The cues for the emotional tenor of the painting lie elsewhere — in the energetic brush marks, the pool of red paint, the sheer ambiguity of the scene. Are we witnessing a passionate encounter, a scene of violence, an injured body, or a medical event? A detail at the center of the painting suggests it could be all of these: a circle and a line, easily missed amid the drips and brushstrokes, come into focus as a stoma, tube, and urostomy bag — revealing this as a frank portrayal of Emin's body after bladder cancer surgery in 2020.

The painting, one of nineteen on view in *Tracey Emin: I Loved You Until The Morning*, is representative of the artist's unusual candor. Emin has always served as her own richest subject matter, taking things as seemingly prosaic as a urostomy bag — or, as in other works, a crumpled cigarette packet, an unmade bed, a pregnancy-test kit — and giving them an artistic form that reveals their untold complexities. Far from claiming to live an exceptional life, Emin has made it her project to break the social taboos and contract of silence that surround the routine messiness of human experience, turning them into the subjects of her art. Through her expressive idiom, she brings to light the unique and deeply personal repercussions that unfold from everyday life — and not just her own.

Although Emin began as a painter — and works primarily as a painter today — a significant portion of her career was defined by an adventurous use of non-traditional media: installations, sculptural assemblages, found objects, memorabilia, appliqué and embroidered textiles, writing, neon, film, and photography. The eclectic modes of her art-making are held together by the dogged consistency of her subject matter, which for three decades has focused with singular tenacity on her own experiences of womanhood and female sexuality. As she processes and reprocesses the emotional residues of memories and events, the work takes whatever material form best captures what she seeks to express. Since 2007 that material form has increasingly been paint on canvas.

Emin's unwavering attention to the intimate details of familiar experiences has made her work legible to an audience far beyond the rarefied art world. Her work, she recognizes, is "really easy to understand."[1] This universality and accessibility has undoubtedly contributed to her popular ascent, especially in Britain, where she is a household name with a public presence and media profile uncommon for an artist in the twenty-first century. "The general public, who don't normally go to art galleries, are much more aware of what I do," she has said.[2] But the same diaristic and confessional components of her work responsible for its broad appeal have, on the flipside, complicated her critical reception and place within the art establishment. Critics, many of them in the popular press, have routinely — and willfully — mistaken her work for unmediated autobiography, accusing her of narcissism, a desire to shock, and an obsession with publicity and fame. So long as Emin's art seemed to mirror her "messy" life, they could ignore the serious subjects of her work.

Yet reducing the work to simple autobiography ignores the vision and complex creativity entailed in translating the experiential into a form that transcends the personal and gives universal expression to the experience of being a woman. In fact, it is only as art that the ordinary circumstances of Emin's life can have any currency — had Emin not made art about them, her life, and she as a person, would have no visibility at all. By transforming her life into art, Emin has broken the mold of what it takes for an artist and a woman to succeed. She offers not simply a political commentary on opportunity, equity, and who gets an art education; she has rewritten that script and put "Mad Tracey from Margate," as she has described herself, into art's "fucking epicenter."[3]

Emin did not enter the art world easily. Her background was unfavorable to an artistic career. Growing up in Margate, then a rundown seaside town, her childhood was marked by spells of poverty and homelessness. She was sexually abused as a child and raped as a teen, leaving school at thirteen and joining a dismal statistic of working-class youth in Britain dropping out of school with no qualifications. As she recounted in her film *How It Feels* in 1996, "I spent all my life fighting against what I should have been. Where I grew up, by the time you were 17 you had one or two kids."[4] With few prospects, but refusing to be limited by her circumstances, Emin spent her youth exploring her sexuality, sewing her own clothes, entering dancing competitions, and envisioning a future beyond the small-town limitations of Margate.

Against all expectation, she got herself an education. In 1980 she lied about her schooling to get on a foundation course at Medway College, in Kent, near Margate. Unable to produce her certificates, she reluctantly took the next best offer, a fashion BTEC—a vocational diploma recently introduced to address the widening educational gap among lower-income families. Learning to sew but uninterested in a fashion career, she determinedly pursued her desire to study art, finally enrolling in London's Sir John Cass School of Art (now the School of Art, Architecture and Design at London Metropolitan University) after overhearing it required no qualifications. She built a portfolio and gained entry to a degree at Maidstone College of Art in Kent, finishing with first-class honors in fine art printmaking, a source of immense pride for her. She took a year off and in 1987 applied for an MA in painting at the prestigious Royal College of Art; she won her place, as she later recalled, on the strength of her sketchbooks and her honest desire to learn how to paint.[5]

To support herself during her MA, Emin worked odd jobs—at a catering firm, staffing a cloakroom, and at the college—and received a hardship fund.[6] For a time, she struggled to meet the requirements of the Royal College but then caught the attention of her tutors, the painters Ken Kiff and Alan Miller, who spent the summer of 1988 teaching her how to paint: "I learned how to stretch canvases, make stretchers, and I learned everything I possibly could in a summer about oil paint and how to paint. And that is a skill."[7] Her 1988 painting *Me & My Nan* (fig. 1), shows Emin applying her new technical understanding of materials and colors to a visual aesthetic that emulated the expressionist style of Edvard Munch and Egon Schiele, artists she had admired since her teens. If the painting appears stylistically distant from Emin's mature work, it is nevertheless striking that its subject—underlined by the vernacular directness of the title—already expresses the deeply personal and autobiographical sentiments of the artist we know today.

While Emin credits her Royal College years as formative ("what I got from being there is my life. I am a painter. And that's where I learned to paint"),[8] she

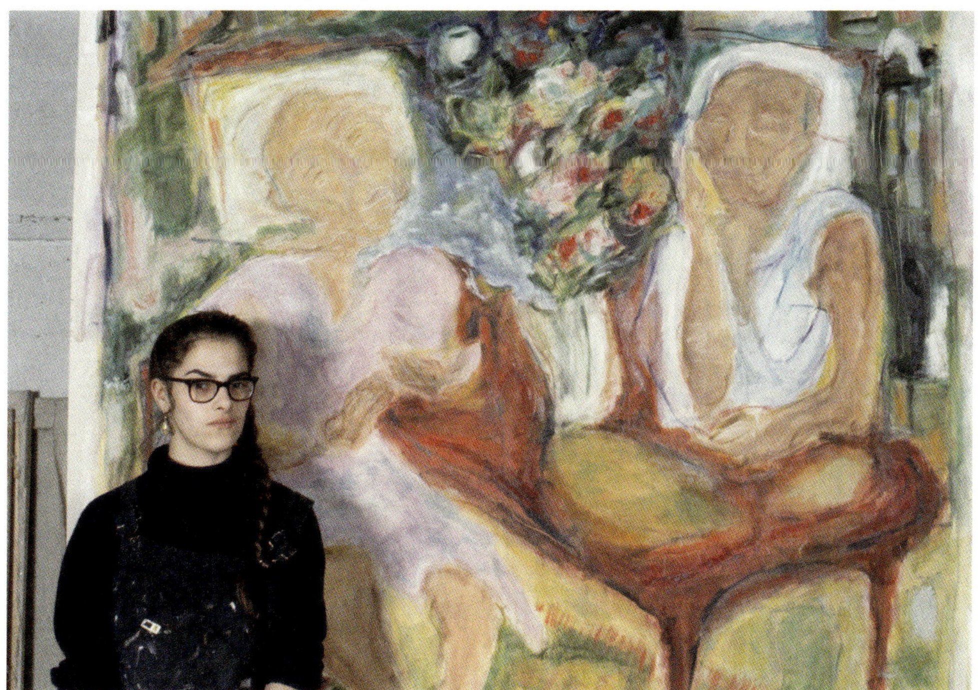

FIG. 1 Tracey Emin with *Me & My Nan* (1988; no longer extant), at the Royal College of Art, London, 1989

acknowledges that she was "in a backwater of art;" her "big figurative paintings . . . seemed so old fashioned" and were "not taken seriously."[9] Halfway through her degree, in frustration, she took her paintings into the courtyard of the Royal College and violently destroyed them, an action she later said "came out of frustration with myself. My only regret was never having it on film. I used a sledgehammer and my paintings were on wood. I went ballistic slashing the sledgehammer around and no one could get near me. And it was simply because I had nowhere to put my paintings so they had to go. That was a mark of my own failure."[10]

With this energetic ceremony, Emin marked the demise of a trajectory and cleared the way for something new. It was the first in a series of extraordinary interventions into her life and work that Emin would take to disrupt and confront her evolving relationship with painting and being an artist.

PAINTING-FAILURE, FAILURE-PAINTING

In 1990, Emin became pregnant, an event that proved cataclysmic to her sense of self and feelings about art. Finding her heightened senses repelled by the smell of oil paint and solvents, she discarded her remaining canvases in the trash and abandoned painting altogether. The prospect of single motherhood, social housing, and poverty — precisely, she later affirmed, the "destiny you've never chosen and everything you'd always fought against all your life" — led her to seek an abortion.[11] The decision put in motion a harrowing process of existential choices, institutional procedures, and loss of bodily autonomy — from a doctor's refusal to sign her referral to a botched termination that ended in septicemia and a traumatic medical intervention. Feeling her body and her art materials conspiring to physically intervene in her efforts to paint, she cut herself off from people she knew and withdrew from the world. Painting became "completely bound up with failure,"[12] leading Emin to an existential low point that almost marked the end of her artistic trajectory: "I gave up painting, I gave up art, I gave up believing, I gave up faith. I had what I called my Emotional Suicide."[13]

The abortion represented a sudden interruption in an otherwise exemplary educational path that, against all odds, had equipped Emin with an astonishingly broad skill set in studio crafts — sewing, embroidery, drawing, printmaking, photography, as well as all the practical applications of painting, from mixing colors to making stretchers and priming canvases. She found herself with all the tools of her trade but with no direction, no confidence, and no desire to apply them. Emin nevertheless utilized her time with resolve and determination to stay close to art. She embarked on a philosophy course and educated herself about the art world, visiting museums, seeing exhibitions, and attending gallery openings. Having abandoned art-making for all intents and purposes, she nevertheless began to participate in the art world more than ever.

The early 1990s thus saw Emin adjacent to the art world — making friends, building a network. By 1992 she began to make forays to get inside. With spirited innovation, she drew up a subscriber scheme, inviting some eighty individuals to invest in her "creative potential" for £10. In return for sending money in the mail, her patrons received handwritten letters detailing intimate stories about Emin's personal experiences — thus beginning the process of channeling the power of her words and distinctive handwriting to connect with her audiences.

In 1993 Emin turned a corner. Her prescient investment scheme paid dividends when one of her subscribers, the gallerist Jay Jopling, offered her a solo show at his new White Cube gallery. With the acute self-awareness that would come to define Emin as an artist, she devised an exhibition that celebrated the ordinariness of her life and her failed trajectory as an artist. Calling it *My Major Retrospective 1963–1993*, she filled the gallery with personal memorabilia and text-based works: her teenage diaries, which visitors could pick up and read; a poignant letter to her uncle who had died in a car crash; and personal family photos. Among the works on view was *Hotel International*, a large, text-based appliqué textile chronicling her life in Margate and named after her family home. On a set of slender, wall-mounted shelves, Emin displayed tiny photographs of the student paintings she had destroyed, each image fixed to a scrap cut from the last piece of canvas she had purchased before her abortion (figs. 2A & B).

The exhibition was well received critically and for Emin marked a path back to art on a self-driven course. The following year she self-published a limited edition of her memoirs, chronicling her life from her birth to her rape at age thirteen, and used the money from her sales to fund a book tour across America. In 1995 she revamped her subscriber initiative with the more official-sounding Emin Bonds, stamped prints issued in denominations of £50 and £500 and redeemable for Emin artworks. She also opened the Tracey Emin Museum in a south London storefront, where she made and displayed her art and held screenings of her films. For the museum's facade, she fabricated an electric neon sign in her own scrawling cursive, the first of the handwritten neons that would become a key strand in her work. Mimicking the traditional mechanisms by which successful artists enter the canon, Emin's remarkable series of projects proved an unorthodox but effective means to carve out her place in the art world.

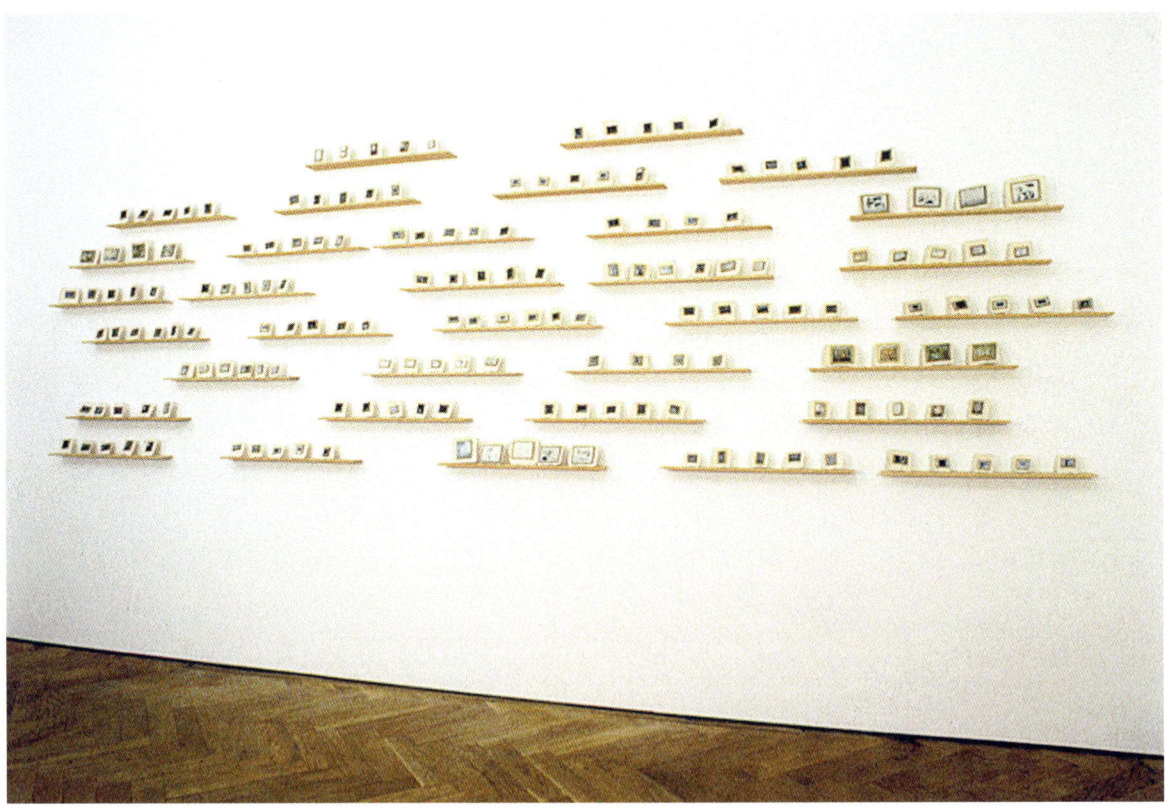

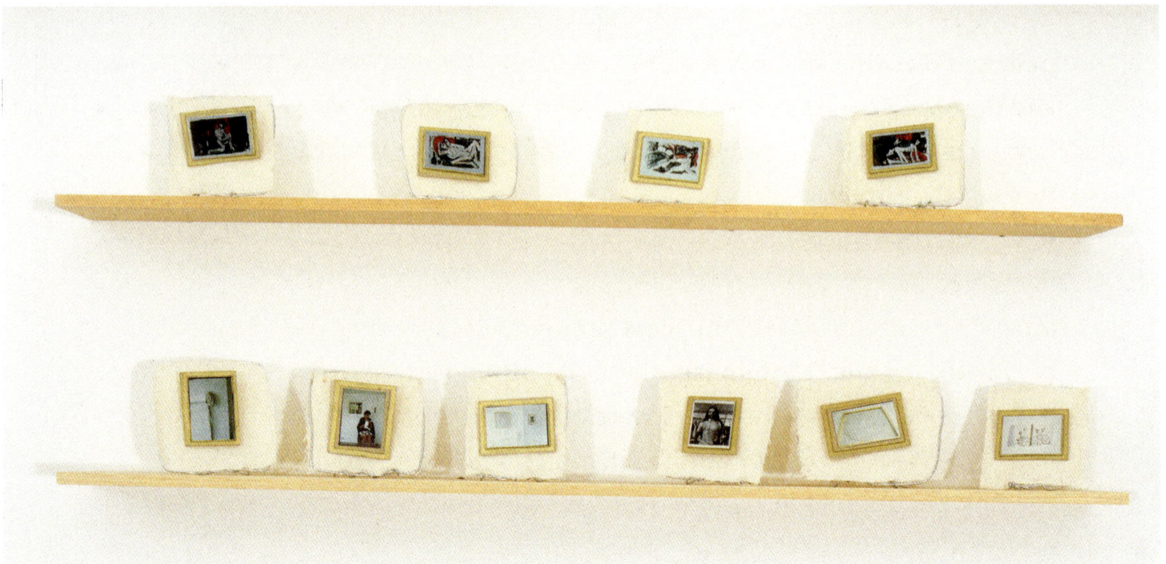

FIGS. 2A & B *My Major Retrospective 1982–1992*, 1993. Installation view and detail from the exhibition *My Major Retrospective 1963–1993,* White Cube, Duke Street, London, 1993. Private collection

In the mid-1990s Emin began to recognize her pregnancy and abortion as experiences inextricably bound to her self-understanding as an artist. In an outpouring of works taking a variety of forms — film, photography, writing, printmaking, and drawing — Emin consciously engaged herself as an artist and a woman, articulating the incalculable consequences of an abortion, details that are often unspoken or obfuscated in the abstract spheres in which debates about reproductive rights take place.

In the twenty-two-minute film *How It Feels* (1996), Emin walks the London streets, revisiting both the office of the doctor who refused to sign her papers and the clinic where she terminated her pregnancy (figs. 3A–F). Along the way, a voice offscreen asks questions, which Emin answers forthrightly and in exacting detail. What emerges is an excruciating catalogue of the circumstances that preceded, accompanied, and followed the botched procedure, including the intolerable pain and bleeding she suffered afterward, the doctor's dismissal of her distress, and the harrowing taxi ride to the emergency room. Abortion, the film conveys, is neither a private event nor a self-contained one. On the contrary, it is an interaction with institutions of power: when a woman simply asks for one, an immense social, economic, medical, and legislative framework is activated and bears down on her. Although for Emin the reverberations of this interaction endured long after the procedure itself, the most profound consequences emerged from the life it afforded her. "My film is really about making art," she observed years later, a statement that makes a stark inversion of conception and termination: pregnancy stood for the end of Emin's art, and abortion came to mean its survival.[14]

Emin continued to explore the larger ramifications of these experiences in subsequent works. *The History of Painting* (1999), one of her most overtly political pieces, consists of four vitrines housing used tampons and a set of framed works containing three pregnancy test strips and a box of morning-after pills (figs. 4A & B). A handwritten text accompanying the assemblage presents the "history of painting" as a history of Emin's menstrual cycles. With a deadpan

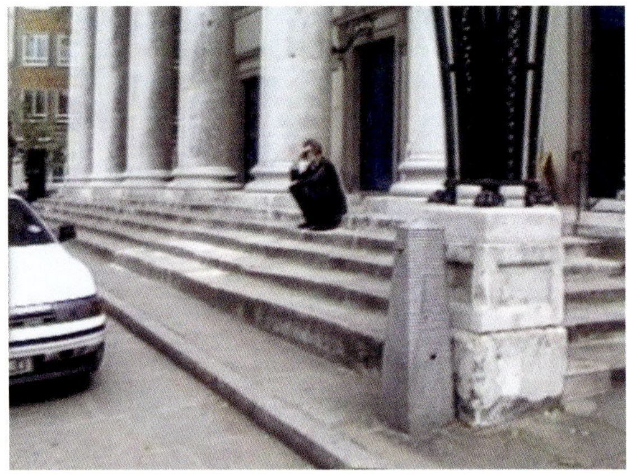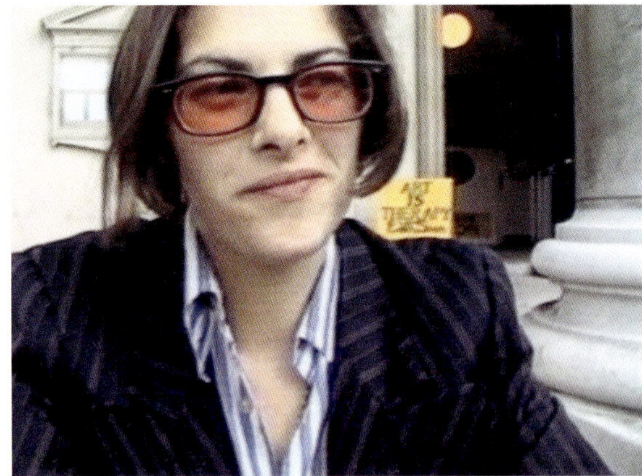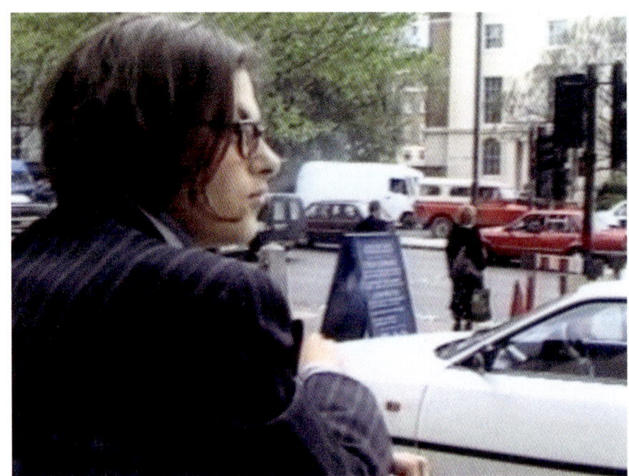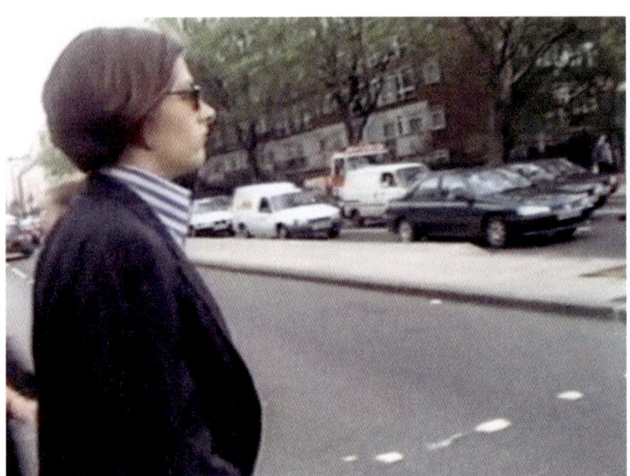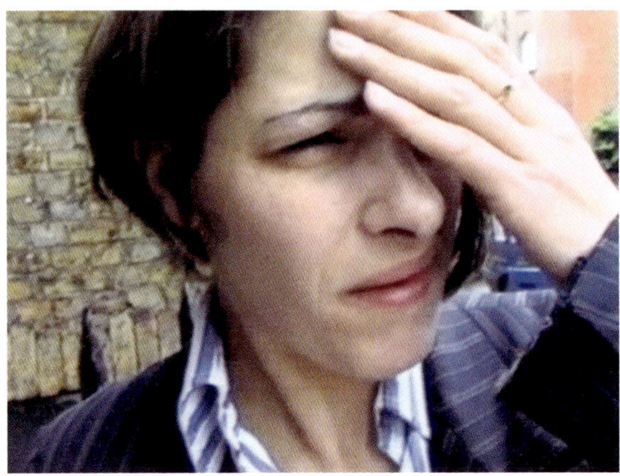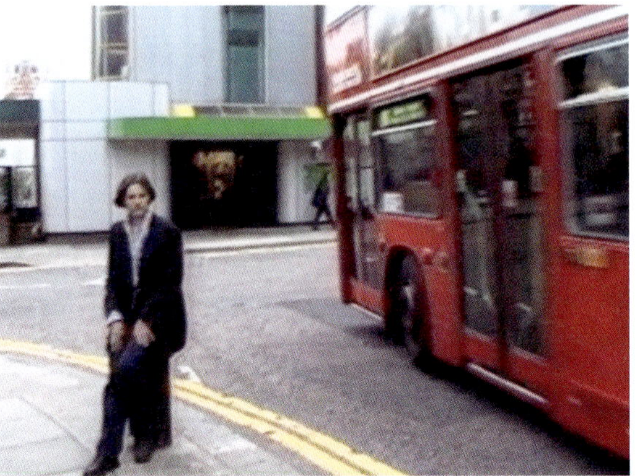

FIGS. 3A–F Stills from *How It Feels*, 1996. Single-channel video, 22 minutes, 33 seconds

sense of comedy, Emin attempts to calculate the number of periods she has had in her life, before giving up. ("It's too complicated.") A tampon signals not being pregnant; the test strips and the morning after pill allude to the possibility of being pregnant and the ensuing range of extreme emotions (fear, dread, desire). Together these components present a sample in time of Emin's life as she tried to be a painter amid the looming possibility of pregnancy. "All that 23 years of bleeding has helped me to be who I am," Emin wrote at the end of the text. "And there's still a long way to go." Implied is that the history of painting is a history that includes Emin at all only because she chose not to become a single mother.

These events thoroughly shifted Emin's conception of creativity. "I had a greater understanding of where things really came from — and where they actually ended up," she observed toward the end of *How It Feels*. Making art, she continued, could no longer "be about a fuckin' picture. It couldn't be about something visual. It had to be about where it was really coming from." Painting had become moribund and redundant, an "old-fashioned idea that made no sense for the times we are living in."[15] It matched neither her artistic ambitions nor her profound feelings about creation: having suddenly confronted the "essence of creativity," she was in pursuit of something more fundamentally connected to human experience.[16]

Emin may have abandoned painting in 1990, but, as she later noted, she never "stopped talking about painting, talking about ideas, getting angry about painting."[17] With relentless desire and determination, she kept up a continuous dialogue with the medium, grasping for an approach that would match her newly charged conception of what art should be. As she put it, her work had not yet caught up with her: "I realized that I was much better than anything I had ever made."[18] It is a statement often mistaken for narcissism when in fact it shows remarkable self-awareness, summarizing her ambition to make a kind of art she could not yet define. "I had to create something totally new or not at all."[19]

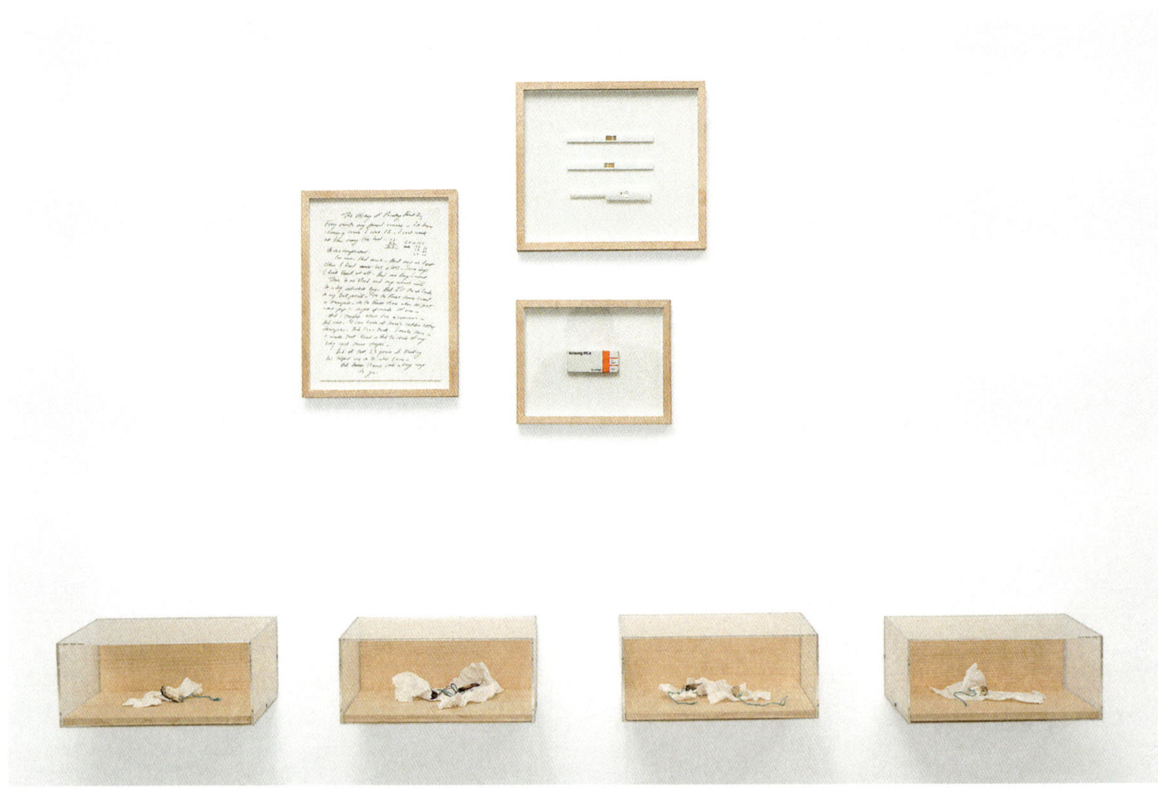

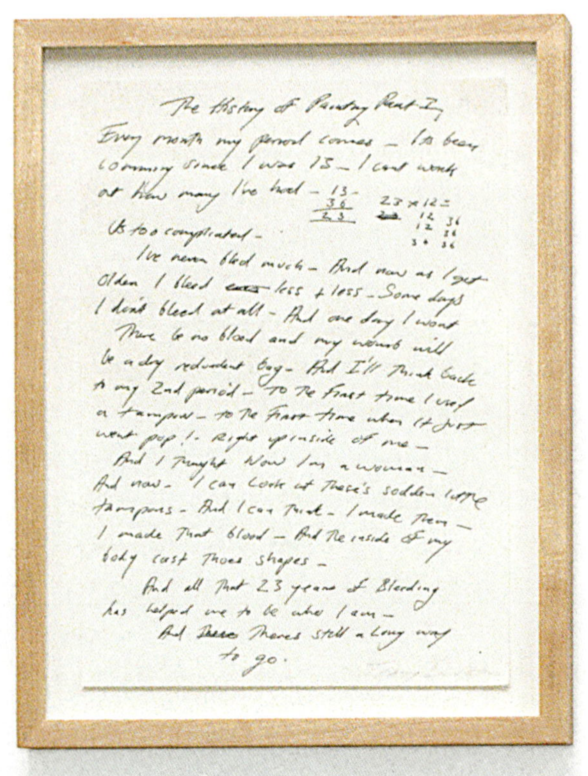

The History of Painting Part I,
Every month my period comes — It's been
Coming since I was 13 — I can't work
out How many I've had — 13 —
  36
  23
It's too complicated —
23 × 12 =
    12 36
    12 36
    3 + 36
  I've never bled much — And now as I get
Older I bleed less + less — Some days
I don't bleed at all — And one day I want
There to be no blood and my womb will
be a dry redundant bag — And I'll think back
to my 2nd period — To the First time I used
a tampon — to the First time when it just
went pop! — Right up inside of me —
  And I thought Now I'm a woman —
And now — I can look at these's sodden little
tampons — And I can think — I made them —
I made That blood — And the inside of my
body cast those shapes —
  And all that 23 years of Bleeding
has helped me to be who I am —
  And There's still a long way
    to go.

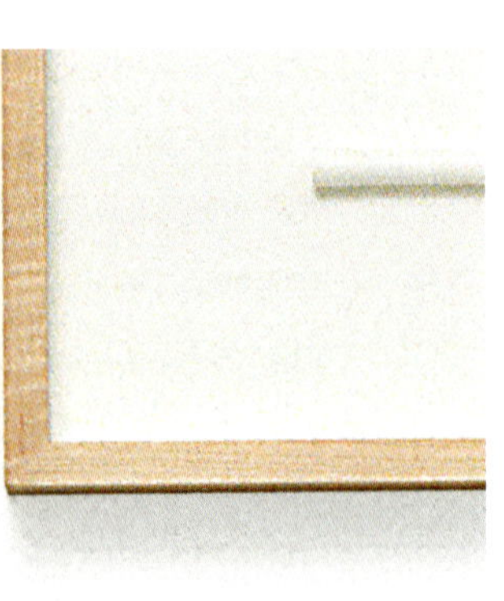

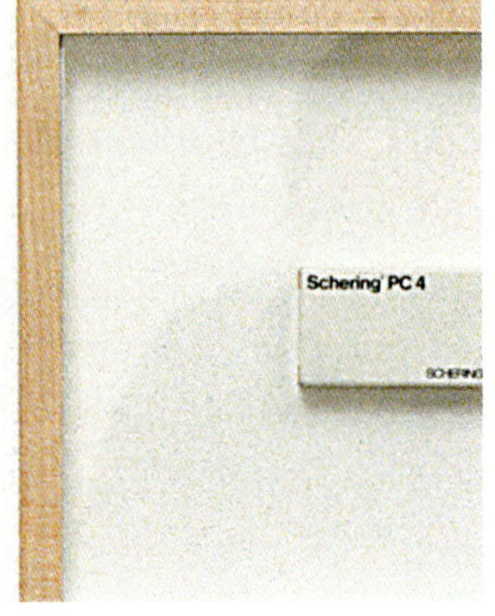

Schering PC 4

AN EXORCISM OF PAINTING

In 1996 Emin orchestrated a three-and-a-half-week confrontation with painting in a gallery in Stockholm. Naked and alone, the artist locked herself in a sparsely furnished studio, its walls fitted with peepholes for gallery visitors to look on as she slept, ate, read newspapers, and painted. She later described her motivation: "There was nothing except a bed, a kettle, a bucket, and some big canvases," she recalled. "There was nothing but me filling the whole room."[20] She chose Stockholm over London because she did not want to be watched by people she knew. The performance, which Emin called *Exorcism of the Last Painting I Ever Made*, was about painting, and specifically the last painting she was working on in 1990 when she became pregnant: a large version of the deposition of Christ that she had discarded during her "emotional suicide." Later she claimed it "was the last time I tried to make a painting as I understood a proper painting was supposed to be."[21]

The exorcism was multifaceted. As Emin explained a few months prior to the performance, she wanted to confront the "emotional entanglement" binding painting to the feelings of guilt and failure generated by her abortion — failure as a human, a woman, and an artist — and to "exorcise those bad feelings."[22] Painting had become "completely bound up with failure. Failure-painting, painting-failure: two things joined together which I wanted to separate."[23] Most of all, the exorcism was a return to "the thing I loved doing the most."[24] The performance was also about her insight and ultimate rejection of certain ways of painting, an exorcism of conventional compositions that emulated the historical expressionist style she admired but that did not match the magnitude of her inner experience. It marked a new pact with the medium.

Photographs of the works made during *Exorcism* show a number of canvases in progress (fig. 5). Remarkably, the paintings Emin made in 1996 bear all the hallmarks of her paintings today. The themes foregrounded are sex, desire, pain, and longing, and the canvases are made with acrylics (Emin never recovered from her aversion to oils). The predominant use of blue, red, black, and white,

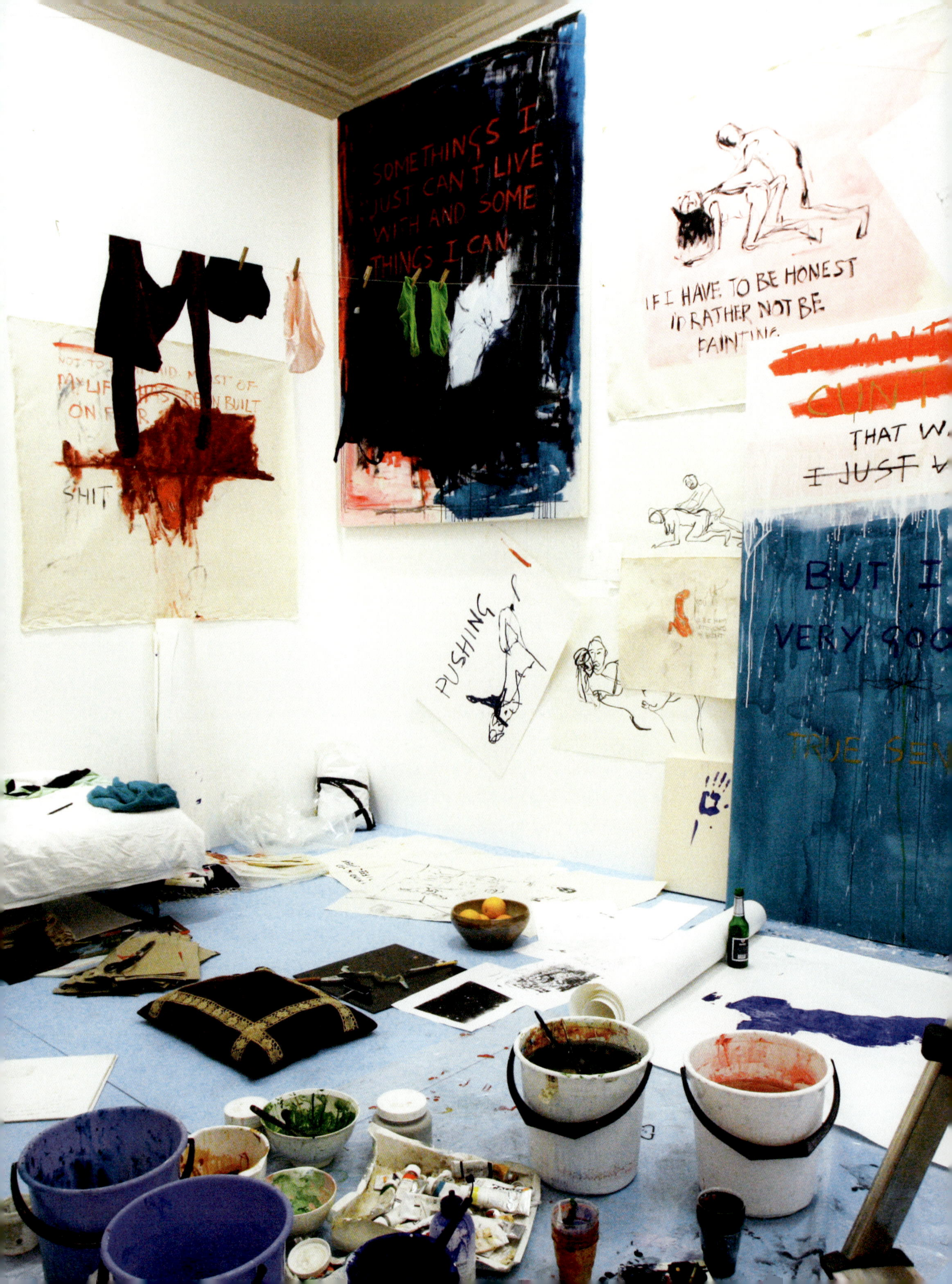
SOMETHINGS I
JUST CAN'T LIVE
WITH AND SOME
THINGS I CAN
IF I HAVE TO BE HONEST
I'D RATHER NOT BE
PAINTING
MY LIFE HAS BEEN BUILT
ON FEAR
SHIT
CUNT
THAT W
I JUST
BUT I
VERY GOO
TRUE SE
PUSHING

the incorporation of text, the outline drawing of the figure, and the repeated overpainting and layering, evocative of the haze of running thought patterns, are all features that have persisted in her work. In one, white paint covering previously worked areas of the canvas has picked up the still-wet red and turned the surface a soft, fleshy pink. The figures — an unabashed, graphic depiction of a couple having sex — were made with Emin's distinct economical brushstrokes, the corrective lines left visible. In another, a torso in white and blue paint can be glimpsed, the rest of the figure obliterated by layers of black. A sentence written in red block letters loudly declares, "SOME THINGS I JUST CAN'T LIVE WITH BUT SOME THINGS I CAN." At the bottom, a corner the black paint does not reach reveals an earlier composition underneath, suggesting the accumulative depths of personal experience and memory.

The works she made in this three-week period could hardly mark a sharper departure from the deposition painting; the exorcism, they signal, was complete: "They all look like Tracey paintings."[25] At the time, Emin did not fully register the success of her confrontation: "My only regret about this project," she said in hindsight, "was that I didn't carry on painting from that moment."[26] Only much later could she see that she had made "great paintings" that matched her desire: "Looking now," she said in 2015, "I can see my enthusiasm for art and everything creative."[27] *Exorcism* was the moment when her art had caught up with her.

A SEMINAL WORK

Exorcism cleared a path for Emin to come "back with a vengeance," as she recently described it, and the next work she made, in 1998, was *My Bed*, an installation in which Emin restaged her own bed as the center of an abject scene frozen in time: dirty sheets, used condoms, soiled underwear, contraceptive packets, empty bottles of alcohol, cigarette ends, and pills, all atop a box frame that functions as a plinth and a stained blue rug (fig. 6).[28] In the work's

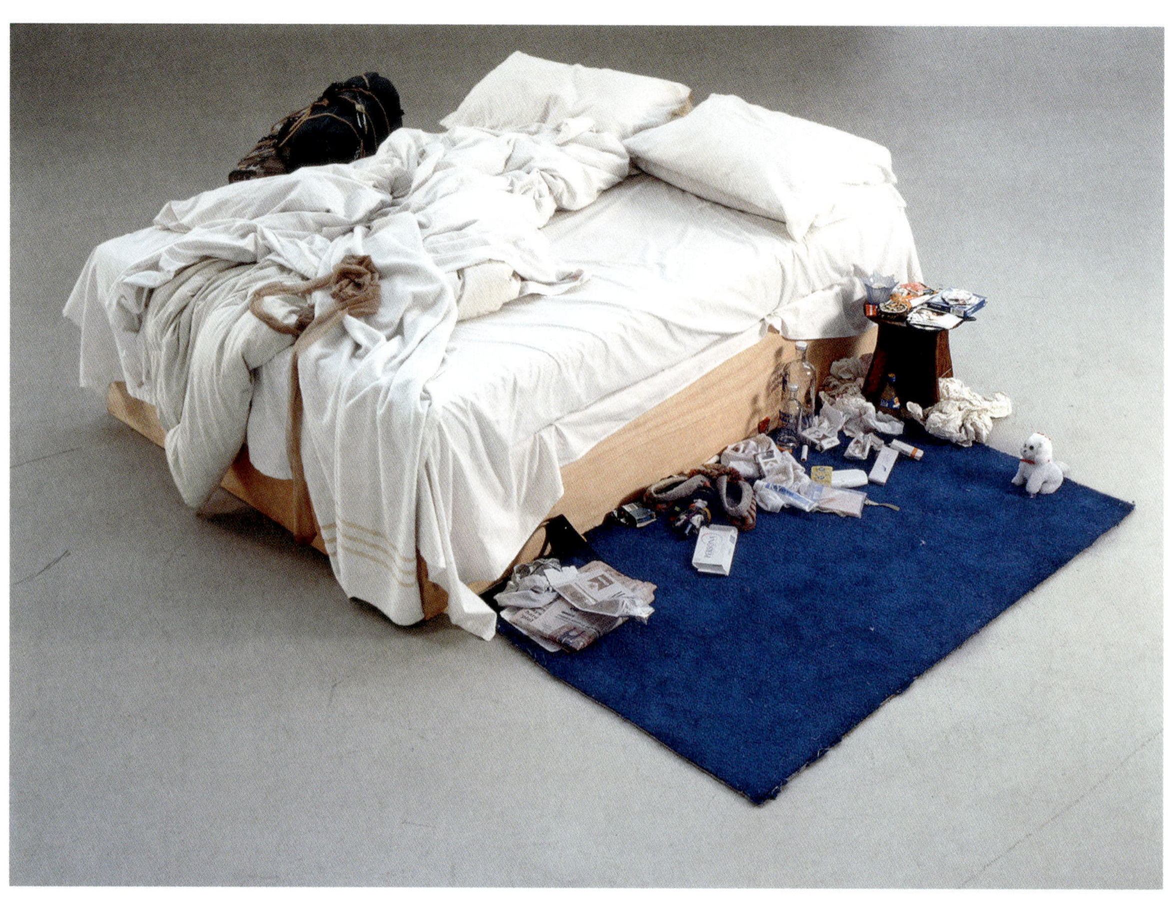

FIG. 6 *My Bed*, 1998. Box frame, mattress, linens, pillows, and various objects, dimensions variable. Tate, London; lent by the Duerckheim Collection on long-term loan

earliest iteration, shown in Tokyo and then in New York, a rope noose was suspended over the scene. The bed, now empty but bearing the trace of Emin's body, conjured lurid, tragic images of what might have occurred — a drunken sexual encounter, loneliness, a slow suicide. It was an idea that emerged from an episode she had herself experienced. "I'd been asleep for days. I'd been drinking excessively. I was a walking disaster . . . at the point of hallucinating," she recalled.[29] Eventually, she got up to drink water and on returning she saw the bed as a place where she could easily have died. In a moment of psychic insight, the bed "suddenly transformed itself into something removed from me, something outside of me, and something beautiful."[30]

Like her sledgehammer action, her emotional suicide, and her exorcism, *My Bed* made a decisive interruption into a downward trajectory and a public pronouncement about death and rebirth: turning her bed into art, detached from herself, meant leaving behind a path to death and choosing her future as an artist. By making a "big, giant, seminal piece of work," she finally had achieved what she needed her work to be, "an extension of me, my soul."[31] Her unreservedly personal success corresponded to a significant acceleration in her public recognition. In 1999 Emin was shortlisted for the Turner Prize and *My Bed* was installed as part of the exhibition at the Tate in London, where it drew enormous crowds. The critical response put her career on sure footing, giving her new freedom as an artist. Yet this was also a moment of increased notoriety, as *My Bed* became sensationalized, consolidating the process by which critics used her work as a way to talk about Emin the person (her dirty bed) rather than Emin the artist. Despite her eloquent expositions on the meaning of *My Bed* — the plinth that made the bed a sculpture, the purposeful theatricality of the scene, her intent to convey the "absolute loneliness" of someone dead for weeks before they were found — critics could only respond with: "But it is literally your bed."[32]

Undeterred by the media's misjudgment of her, Emin developed a finely tuned repertoire using new materials and exhibiting widely both at home and abroad. She turned each new medium in her prolific output into an idiosyncratic artistic expression: neons that reproduced her recognizable handwriting; monoprints characterized by her spindly line, produced by writing backward; appliqué blankets and increasingly sophisticated embroideries that mimicked the line and washes of her watercolor figure studies. It was only in August 2006, when she learned she had been selected to represent Britain at the Venice Biennale, that Emin determined she would return to painting. By then, *Exorcism* was already ten years behind her.

RETURN TO PAINTING

Emin was only the second woman in the history of the British Pavilion at the Biennale to be offered a solo show. She recognized the immensity of the opportunity and the "vast responsibility" that accompanied it.[33] Her decision to make Venice about painting was hardly intuitive. At a time when her reputation was firmly tied to her makeshift craft aesthetic and use of nontraditional media, choosing to make paintings entailed no small professional risk. With the pavilion opening in spring 2007, less than six months away, there also wasn't much time. But, rather than "a best of Emin," she determined to do something that felt meaningful to herself, "something that changed my whole perspective."[34]

Emin rented a space to be used solely for painting and drawing, purchased some thirty canvases, and got to work. She shared her difficulties with the process in her weekly newspaper column in the *Independent*: "The more I struggled with the paintings, the worse they became. I would paint something OK, and then realise OK wasn't good enough. I would then get angry and paint over it. Paint something OK, and know it wasn't good enough."[35] In the end, Emin and Andrea Rose, the commissioner for the British Pavilion, included only three large canvases, completing the presentation with a group of smaller paintings, sculptures, neons, textiles, monoprints, and watercolors (fig. 7).

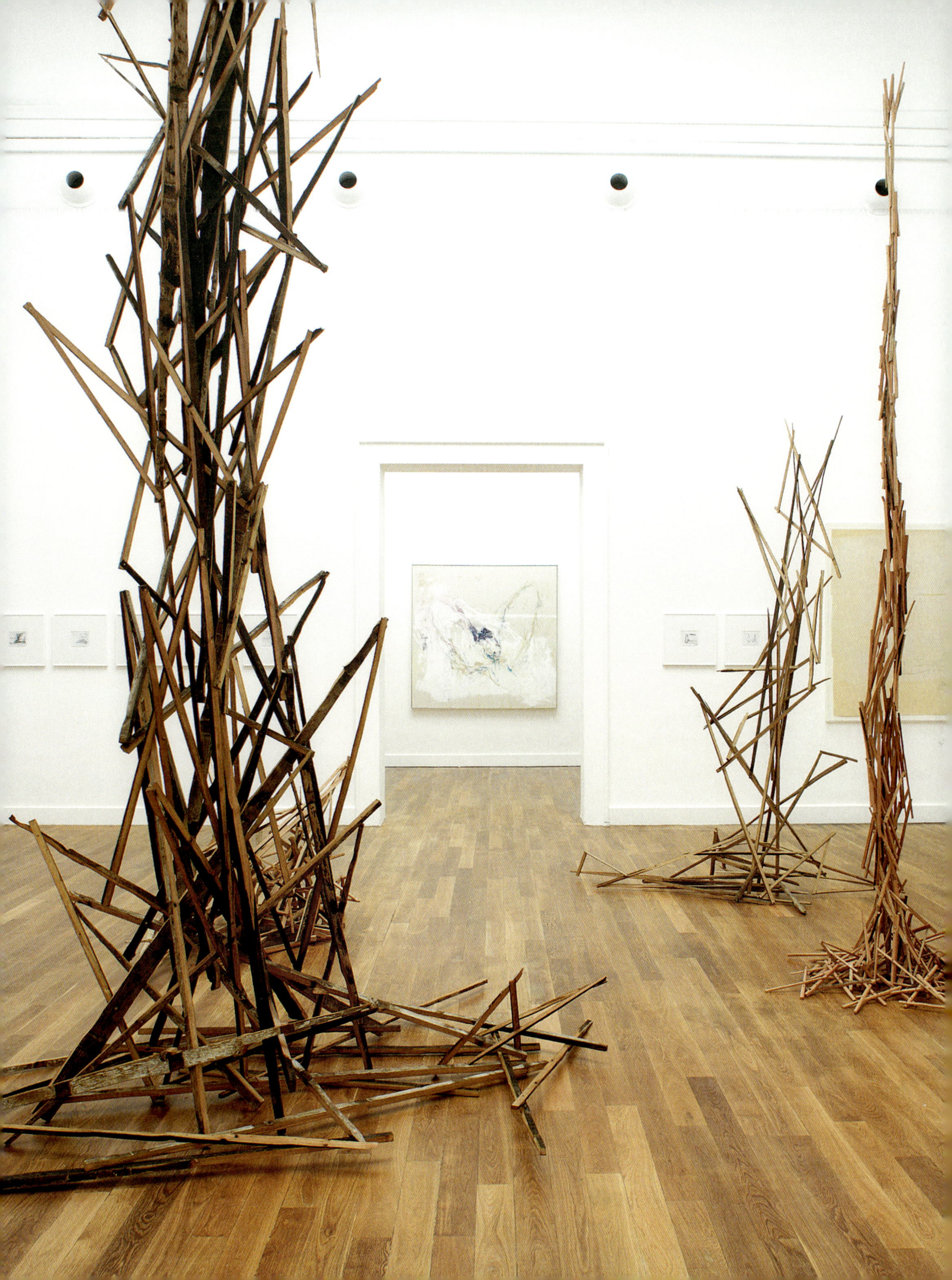

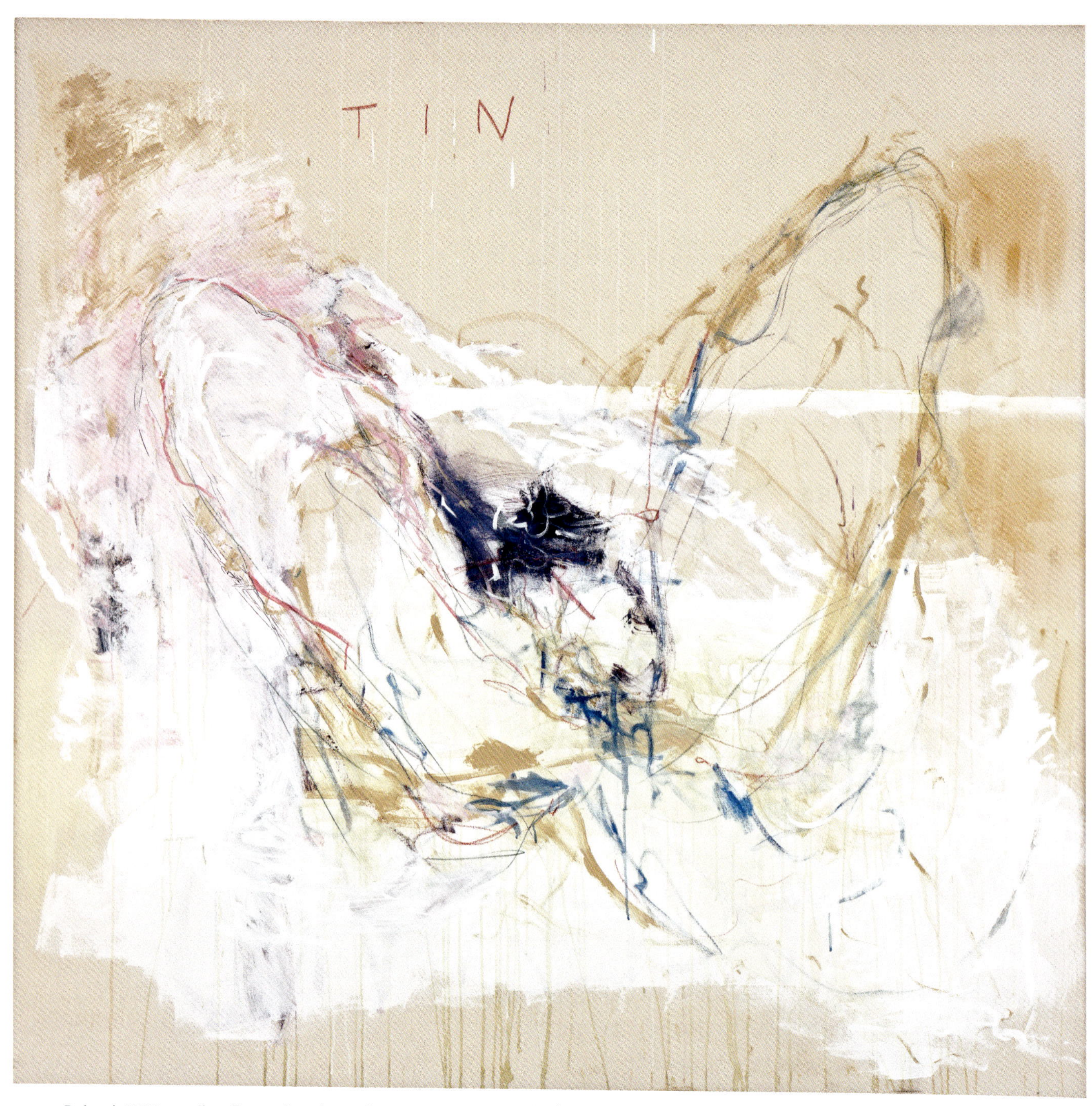

FIG. 8 *Ruined*, 2007, acrylic, oil pastel, and pencil on canvas, 71⅞ x 71⅞ in. (182.5 x 182.5 cm). Private collection

For an audience used to Emin's graphic and direct expressions about sex, abortion, grief, and loss, the subtle and even hesitant qualities of the paintings presented a surprising and unexpected shift. The loosely rendered naked figures and fragments of female anatomy come together in enigmatic scenes. In *Ruined* (2007), quivering lines of paint provide a subtlety that barely gives shape to a partial view of a woman's prone body, her legs drawn up and her genitals exposed (fig. 8). The title invokes a play on an old-fashioned misogynistic term used to describe a woman deemed forever unmarriageable — and thus without future prospects — by having premarital sex. Reducing the body to its sexual parts, the foreshortened image suggests the viewpoint of a gynecologist, a midwife, a doctor, or a partner. The white paint around the body creates an evocation of clean white sheets, but whether they belong to a homely bed, a clinical table, or a hospital environment is unclear. The composition invites the viewer to contemplate all these possibilities.

Venice was not her only forum for showing her paintings that year. In autumn 2007 she opened a large exhibition at Gagosian Gallery in Beverly Hills — a pivotal foray into the blue-chip commercial sphere of the United States. Emin displayed eight large new canvases alongside not only her familiar mediums of embroidery, print, and neon but also a collection of elegiac and ambitious sculptures cast in bronze. Installation views show the paintings anchoring the exhibition and the sculptures dispersed across the floor, a shift toward traditional media not typically associated with Emin's oeuvre (fig. 9). As her first major painting exhibition, the show marked a milestone in her career. If the critical reception was muted, Emin was pleased with the advancement in her work, describing it at the time as "the best show I've ever done."[36]

Overpainting, repainting, obscuring, and covering up are all characteristic of the paintings she was making at this time, with the effect of suggesting veils being drawn across their surfaces. *A rose* (2007; pl. 3), is encrusted with such layering, its soft, muted hues created by white paint picking up the brighter colors of earlier compositions on the same canvas. While working on the painting in her studio

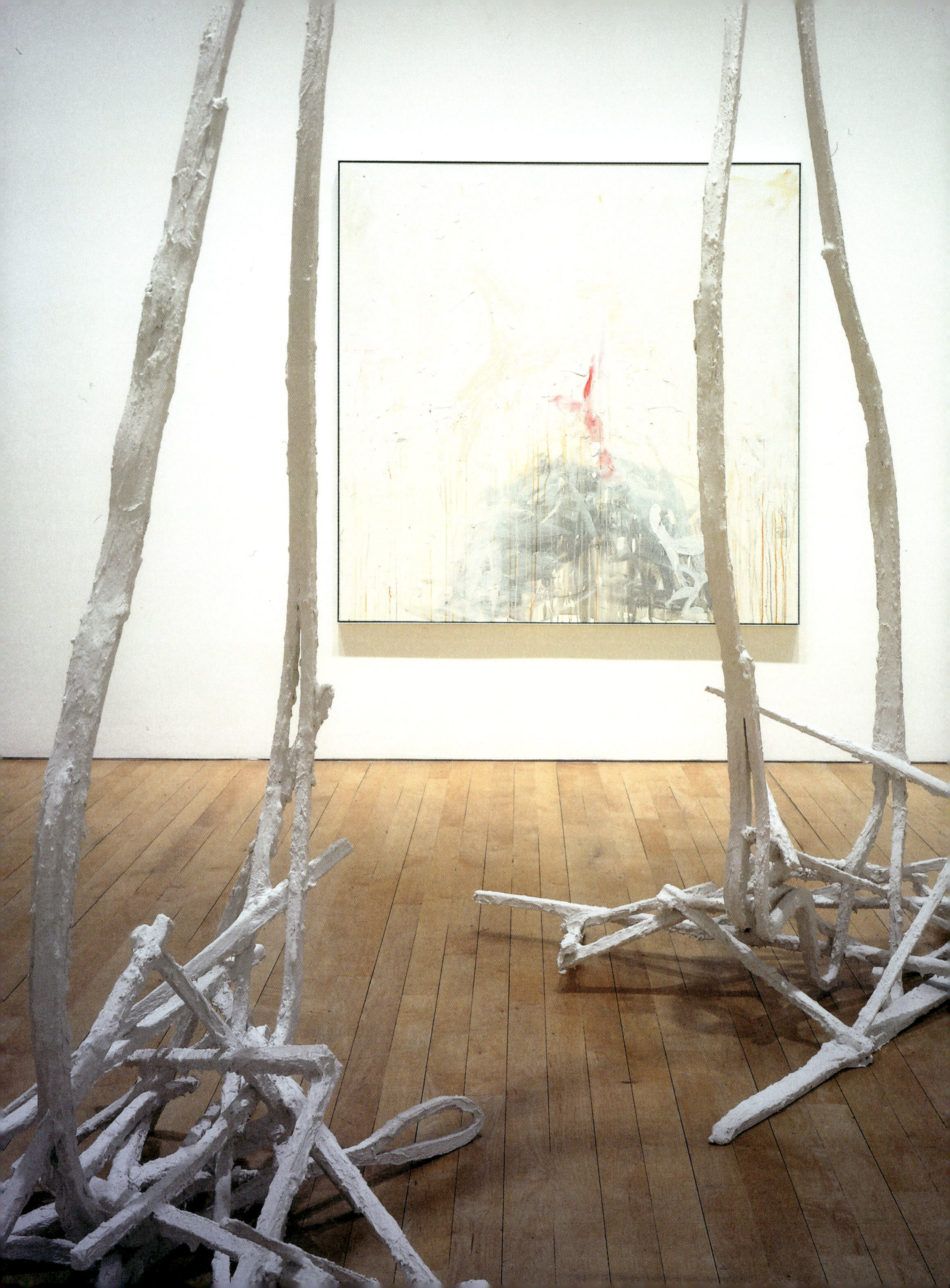

and before giving it a formal title, Emin had called it *Turner Eat Your Heart Out*, seeing it as her version of Turner's stormy atmospheric effects, achieved through the expressive application of paint. The painting nearly forecloses any figurative resemblance or intelligible reading. Yet the faint gray, mound-shaped shadowing at the bottom and the few tangled red lines at the center — suggestive of the "rose" of the title and doubling for a vulva — cohere with unmistakable clarity into a fragment of a woman's body, legs open, in a composition similar to the more overt *Ruined*. Both paintings, in fact, bring to mind Gustave Courbet's *Origin of the World* (1866), a fitting analogy, perhaps, given Emin's own description of the motif as a creation story: "A shape that I invented, a sexual apparition of fecundity, a shape that should have already existed, but only does because of my intervention."[37]

PAINTING NOW

Since Venice, painting has been at the forefront of Emin's art and in many ways her career has come around in a rich full circle. Where once she painstakingly sought to emulate the work of expressionist painters such as Egon Schiele and Edvard Munch, now she is being shown alongside them, in her own unique idiom.[38] With new-found freedom, she prioritizes painting and drawing, while also making sculptures in between, modelled on a small scale and enlarged for casting in bronze. Her journey has also taken her back to her origin in Margate — the small seaside town she escaped as a young woman but that is now her alma mater, her primary residence, the site of her foundation and residency program, and the home of her future legacy — a place that shaped her and that she is now reshaping in turn, reimagining the psychogeography of the town by creating educational opportunities of a kind not on offer to her growing up (fig. 10). Reflecting on her career in a 2019 interview, Emin described her earliest efforts as a gradual "transition *towards* the work, *towards* the artist I was going to be," concluding that "the kind of artist that I am now, this is it, this is me, this is who I am."[39]

The nineteen canvases on view in *Tracey Emin: I Loved You Until The Morning* — the first ever solo show of her paintings in a museum — trace both the consistency Emin brings to her subjects and the development of her mature expression. Spanning from *Pelvis High* (pl. 2), exhibited in Venice in 2007, to the very recent *I Followed you to the end* (2024; pl. 19), the selection illuminates Emin's thorough dedication to fulfilling the ambitious task she set herself back in 1990 — to find a new emotional language for painting. As the ambiguities in her early paintings have often given way to forceful, graphic depictions of the female body as a site of both momentous pain and pleasure, the exhibition also invites us to reevaluate Emin's sophisticated approach to the medium and its relationship to her larger body of work.

The practical parameters of her paintings were established back in 1996 during her exorcism and can be seen across her subsequent output: the use of acrylics rather than oils; a palette dominated by reds and blues, often with an abundant use of white; and a limited set of canvas shapes that she returns to again and again. Her formal repertoire centers on the female body and her words — whether painted on the canvas as an integral part of the composition or in the form of the title, invariably written in pencil on the bottom edge — remain central.

Several distinct visual themes emerge among her paintings. In one, a loosely painted seated, crouching, or reclining figure floats across a horizontal or square picture plane, where it merges with a saturated field of white, red, or black. Of these, *I never Asked to Fall in Love – You made me Feel like This* (2018; pl. 8) is the most vivid. A figure is suspended in a reservoir of red, as though drowning or bathing in blood. Drips of red paint move upward like a living corporeal sub-stance, defying gravity, in turn suggesting that the figure inhabits an unearthly dimension. A darker shape — almost like a crab with giant pincers — sits under-neath her torso and legs, suggesting a threatening presence. *You kept it coming* (2019; pl. 13) is more equivocal, with the line between pleasure and pain less clearly drawn. A female figure kneels on a red floor that has tinged the upper

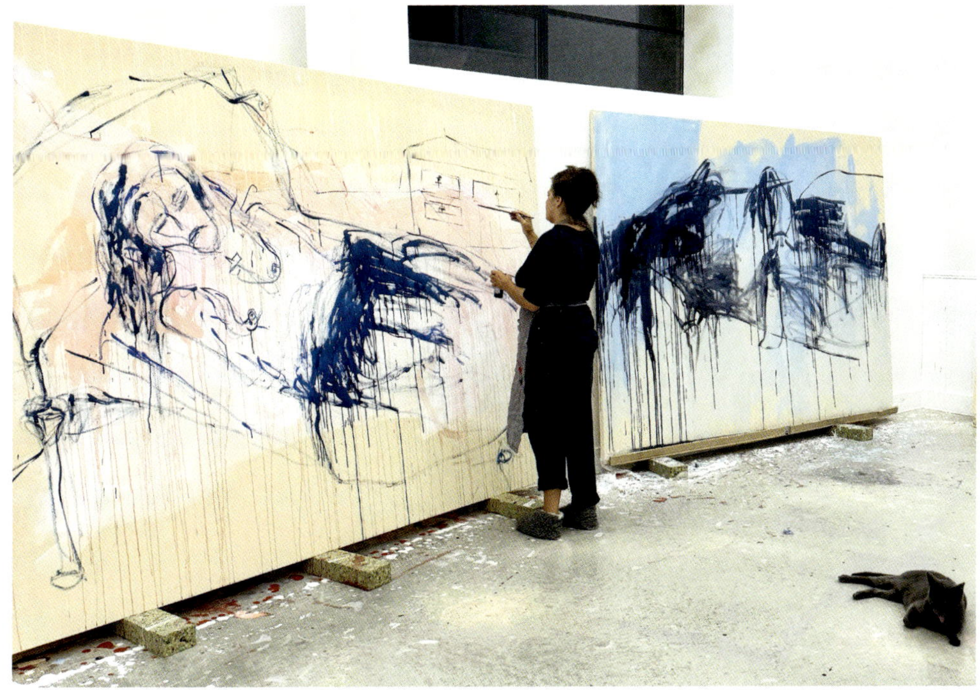

area of white paint with pink hues. An ambiguous shape hovers over the woman, echoing her contours, summoning thoughts of an oppressive weight pushing the woman down or of an aura or spirit creating a protective cover.

This sense of hovering presences recurs in a painting that Emin made after her cancer surgery, pointedly titled *I have to Keep Living* (2022). The outline of a figure lying contorted on an undefined surface is accompanied by a ghostly white shape at her side; rising from her is a spectral echo of her own body, suggesting a departing spirit, a dream, or an out-of-body experience (fig. 11). Amid the chimeric atmosphere created by the layered impasto of the painting, an ominous clinical air hangs over the scene — the green-tinged shape at the back suggests the thick glass of a hospital window, the gray surface below the figure a linoleum floor. As we witness the inner existential experience unfolding for the woman, it is left to our imagination to wonder if she is in a bed, on an operating table, or even on a mortuary slab.

In another distinctive grouping, a vertical format focuses attention on a single standing female figure. One of the earliest paintings of this kind is *Black Cat* (2008; pl. 4), a striking self-portrait inspired by Edgar Allan Poe's disturbing and

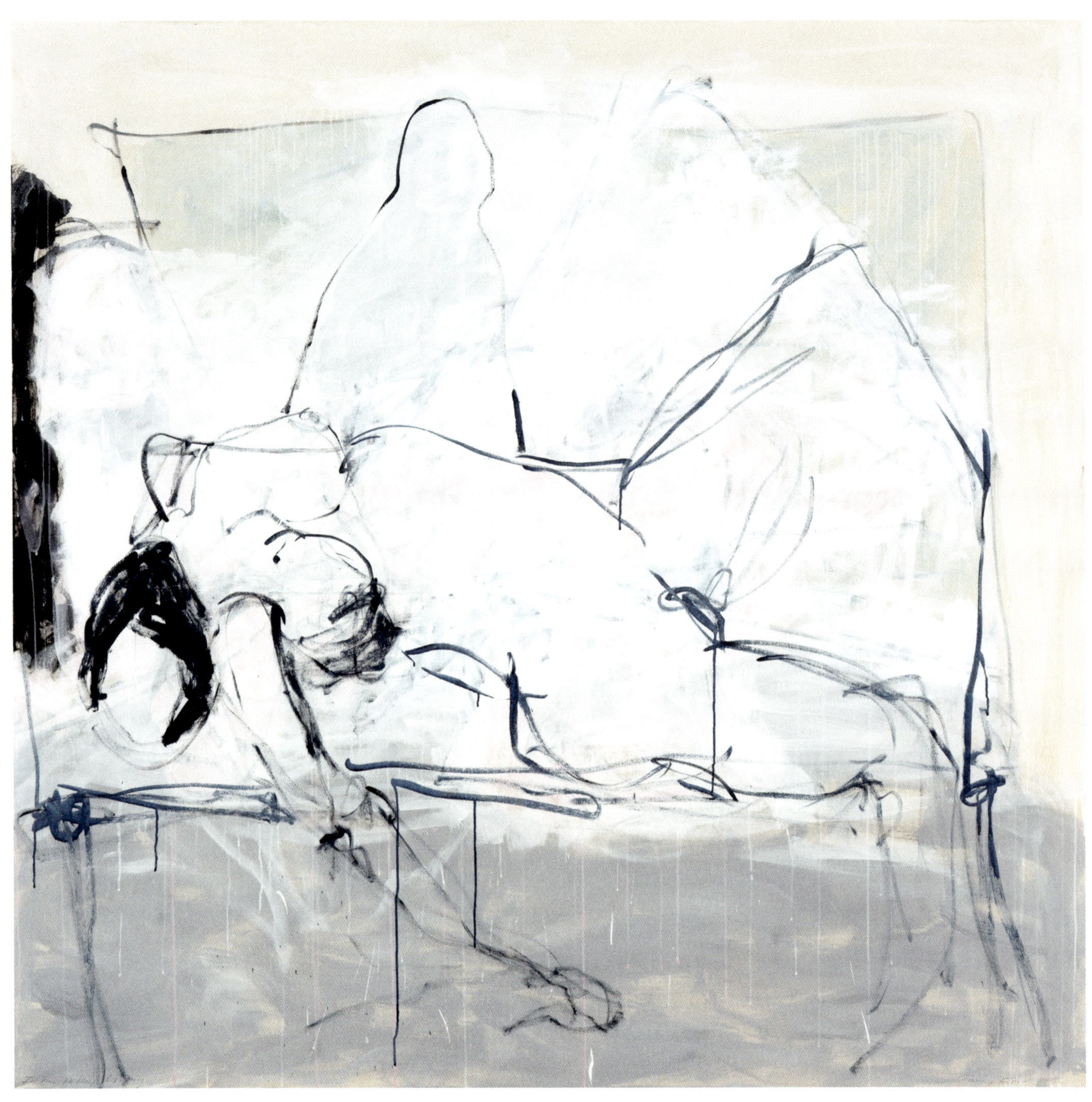

FIG. 11 *I have to Keep Living*, 2022. Acrylic on canvas, 72⅛ x 72¼ in. (183.2 x 183.5 cm). Private collection

violent short story "The Black Cat."[40] Emin (who frequently includes references to her cats in her work) has depicted herself wearing an open black dress, her face completely blacked out. A pool of red paint by her feet suggests the aftermath of an unknown tragedy. Emin described the dualistic quality of the work, which appears on the one hand as "a demonic self-portrait, skittish and psychotic, something heavy and malevolent to behold. On the other hand it could come across as being gothic, cartoonish, something from the Hammer House of Horror."[41] Made over seven years, it began as a landscape before being turned 90 degrees and changed into a portrait, as the horizontal drips of red paint record. The soft pink, yellow, and blue tones of the landscape can be seen through the white, as if in a mist, fusing with the figure. Its layered hues and the long durée of its making demonstrate the personal attachment that Emin develops with her paintings over time.

The leitmotif of the single standing female appears repeatedly in Emin's oeuvre, often on narrower canvases that activate a sense of enclosure around the figure. *I wanted to be clean* (2023; pl. 16) shows a naked figure underneath a shower head, but instead of water a red shroud has been poured around her, like a rinse of blood. Rivulets of red mix with gray and with the outline of her torso before dissolving her lower body into pure paint, as if her effort to "be clean" stands for a purification ritual enacted in an intense painterly field. The putting down of colors and forms and the natural run-off from the wet acrylic allow the action of painting itself to do much of the compositional work on the canvas, a device we also see at work in the most recent paintings in this exhibition, *Don't Ask me to be like you* and *I Followed you to the end* (both 2024; pls. 18 and 19).

Emin's writing, which asks the viewer to spend time with the work, remains a key component in her oeuvre. In *I said No* (pl. 5), begun in 2005 but not completed until 2015, the use of block letters harkens back to Emin's exorcism paintings. The words "I SAID NO," painted in a thin red, are almost obscured by white overpaint. Once seen, the sentence comes through loudly enough, sitting like a headline next to a sparsely delineated naked figure and conjuring up the distinct context of nonconsensual sex. A red pool of color concentrates around the lower torso of the figure, and patches of sunflower yellow suggest a patterned floor or carpet on which she rests. Only on closer looking do these shapes resolve into further text. Some of the letters are merged with other marks, leaving us to fill in the blanks to make out a coherent sentence: "LIKE A NIGHT WHEN I WAS SO DRUNK." The interplay between these two pieces of text creates a sparse narrative in which the words at the top are understood as a spoken command (whether in fact said out loud or not), while those at the bottom appear as a fleeting thought or partial recollection. Word, image, and the layered materiality of the paint create the sense of a memory being examined, turned over, and grasped onto even as it begins to fade.

The use of block letters and obscured words also appears in later works, such as *You Held my Face* (2018; pl. 10), in which the combination of figure, text, and overpaint creates an existential sense of fear, loss, love, and threat. A black cloud marks both the absence and the presence of another figure, leaving behind only the emotional residue — perhaps anger, loss, grief, or all of these at once, as expressed by the words "You Touched," and the overpainted "My Face." The head of the female figure is completely covered in vigorous dark red brushstrokes. Like many of Emin's works, the painting alludes to the wide range of emotions activated by being in love, being left, and the solitary internal turmoil that remains.

The most recent painting in the exhibition, *I Followed you to the end* (2024; pl. 19), can be seen as a summation of Emin's most central subjects and occupations. The canvas alludes to a page in a book or journal, providing a surface for an extended poem or letter in Emin's recognizable cursive handwriting. A woman emerges like an apparition from a field of vibrant red edged by black shadows and a circle reminiscent of the blood moon in a total lunar eclipse. Although her face is obscured, she brings an intensity of address, as if moving forward to engage the viewer in her incantation or spell casting. Her lower body dissolves to clear a space for words, which are written on the bare canvas in the same black of which her body is composed: "You made me like this. All of You — You — You men that I so insanely loved so much. You are the ones that made me feel so alone. All of you — each of you in your individual way. I — I — I — was at fault to keep loving you. Like a fool I followed love to the end. Like the sad haunted soul that I am, I followed you to the end." She ends her lament to past lovers by putting the words "THE END" on a new line in capital letters — like the final flourish that comes on the last page of a fairy tale.

A UNIVERSAL LANGUAGE

Over the years, Emin has repeatedly pointed out that to make work from an individual perspective is hardly unusual and in fact relates to a long-standing tradition in the history of art: "Van Gogh did that, Edvard Munch did that, Rembrandt did that. It's not a new thing."[42] What these artists share in common — and a component of what makes their work so potent — is their capacity to develop that simple notion into a uniquely personal expression that nevertheless conveys momentous universal ideas. Throughout her career Emin has had to defend this same approach, reminding critics that the significance of her work is its capacity to "transcend the personal."[43] This speaks volumes about the way the public responds to women's experiences — that is, overlooking and belittling due to the culturally dominant attitudes of the time. Although many of her subjects have lately emerged in topical public discourses, the personal, prosaic, and complicated ramifications of these experiences are still rarely given full public expression. Sexual abuse, abortion, female sexuality, and more recently the profound physical consequences of living with a stoma — these are all subjects about which Emin has "always had a voice," but only recently, by her own estimation, do "people realize, actually, I'm talking a qualified language about being a woman and how women are treated." It's a language, she insists, that "shouldn't be my language. This is a universal language that people have to start talking."[44]

NOTES

In writing this essay, I am grateful to Harry Weller for our many conversations; to Nick Mead for reading and commenting on multiple drafts; and to Honey Luard for helping me conceptualize the book as a whole.

1. Tracey Emin, in conversation with Philip Larratt-Smith, "Histoire de Tracey Emin," in Philip Larratt-Smith, *Tracey Emin, How It Feels* (Buenos Aires: Editorial Oceano Argentina S.A, 2012), 101.

2. Larratt-Smith, "Histoire de Tracey Emin," 101.

3. Larratt-Smith, "Histoire de Tracey Emin," 99.

4. From *How It Feels* (1996), film script reprinted in *Tracey Emin, Works 1963–2006* (New York: Rizzoli, 2006), 64.

5. Tracey Emin, "My Life in a Column," *The Independent*, January 22, 2009. Reprinted in the collection of weekly columns from 2005 to 2009, *My Life in a Column* (New York: Rizzoli, 2011), 355–57.

6. "Artist Tracey Emin CBE, RA (MA Painting, 1989) on her time at the College," November 1, 2012, rca.ac.uk/news-and-events/news/tracey-emin/.

7. "What Makes an Artist: Tracey Emin," Royal College of Art, November 1, 2012, vimeo .com/315246053/e818a47081.

8. "What Makes an Artist: Tracey Emin."

9. "Tracey Emin in Conversation with Carl Freedman," in *Tracey Emin: I Cried Because I Love You* (Hong Kong: Lehmann Maupin and White Cube, 2016), 10.

10. "Artist Tracey Emin CBE, RA (MA Painting, 1989)."

11. *Works 1963–2006*, 62.

12. Tracey Emin, interview with Jean Wainwright, in *The Art of Tracey Emin* (London: Thames & Hudson, 2002), 198.

13. Wainwright interview, 64.

14. Larratt-Smith, "Histoire de Tracey Emin," 77.

15. *Works 1963–2006*, 67.

16. Tracey Emin, interview with Melvin Bragg, *The South Bank Show*, ITV, August 19, 2001, 24 min., www.youtube.com/watch?v=XQlniTSTEZo.

17. "Tracey Emin in conversation with Carl Freedman," 10.

18. Bragg interview, 27 min.

19. Bragg interview, 24 min.

20. Tracey Emin in conversation with Carl Freedman, "Break on Through to the Other Side," in *Tracey Emin, Works 1963–2006* (New York: Rizzoli, 2006), 255.

21. Freedman, "Break on Through," 255.

22. Tracey Emin, interview with Carl Freedman, *Minky Manky* (London: South London Gallery, 1995), unpaginated.

23. Wainwright interview, 198.

24. "Tracey Emin: Exorcism of the Last Painting I Ever Made at Faurschou New York," press release, September 2023, Farschou gallery, New York.

25. Tracey Emin, interview with Courtney J. Martin, in this volume, 112.

26. "Tracey Emin: Exorcism of the Last Painting I Ever Made."

27. Mark Brown, "Emin's breakthrough Exorcism goes up for auction," *Guardian* (London), January 22, 2015, 7.

28. Martin interview, 113.

29. Freedman, "Break on Through," 252.

30. Freedman, "Break on Through," 252.

31. Martin interview, 113.

32. Tracey Emin, interview with Nicholas Glass, "Uncut Tracey Emin Interview on 'My Bed' (1999)," ITN Archive, 1 min. 50 sec., youtube.com/watch?v=ADGhLpUzSfQ.

33. Emin, "My Life in a Column," October 20, 2006, reprinted in *My Life in a Column*, 154.

34. Claire Armstrong, "Tracey Emin, A Good Year," *Art World* (Australia), Issue 3, March/April 2008, 46.

35. "Welcome to my world; Tracey Emin at the Venice Biennale" *The Independent* (London), June 7, 2007.

36. Armstrong, "A Good Year," 46.

37. Tracey Emin, "You Left Me Breathing," in *You Left Me Breathing* (Beverly Hills, CA: Gagosian Gallery, 2007), 43.

38. *Where I want to go. Tracey Emin, Egon Schiele*, Leopold Museum, Vienna, 2015; *Tracey Emin/Edvard Munch: The Loneliness of the Soul*, Royal Academy, London, 2019, and Munch Museum, Oslo, 2021.

39. "Tracey Emin CBE," Art Talk podcast, Season 1, Episode 8, March 28, 2019, 7 min.

40. Emin made the painting for an exhibition about art inspired by Edgar Allan Poe, curated by the artist Harland Miller: *You Dig the Tunnel, I'll Hide the Soil*, White Cube, London, 2008.

41. Tracey Emin, "My Life in a Column," April 4, 2008, reprinted in *My Life in a Column*, 302.

42. Tracey Emin, interview with Kathleen Bühler, *Magazin: Tracey Emin 20 years* (Kunstmuseum Bern, 2008), 181.

43. Bühler interview, 181.

44. "Tracey Emin CBE," 43 min.

PAINTINGS

Plates 1–19

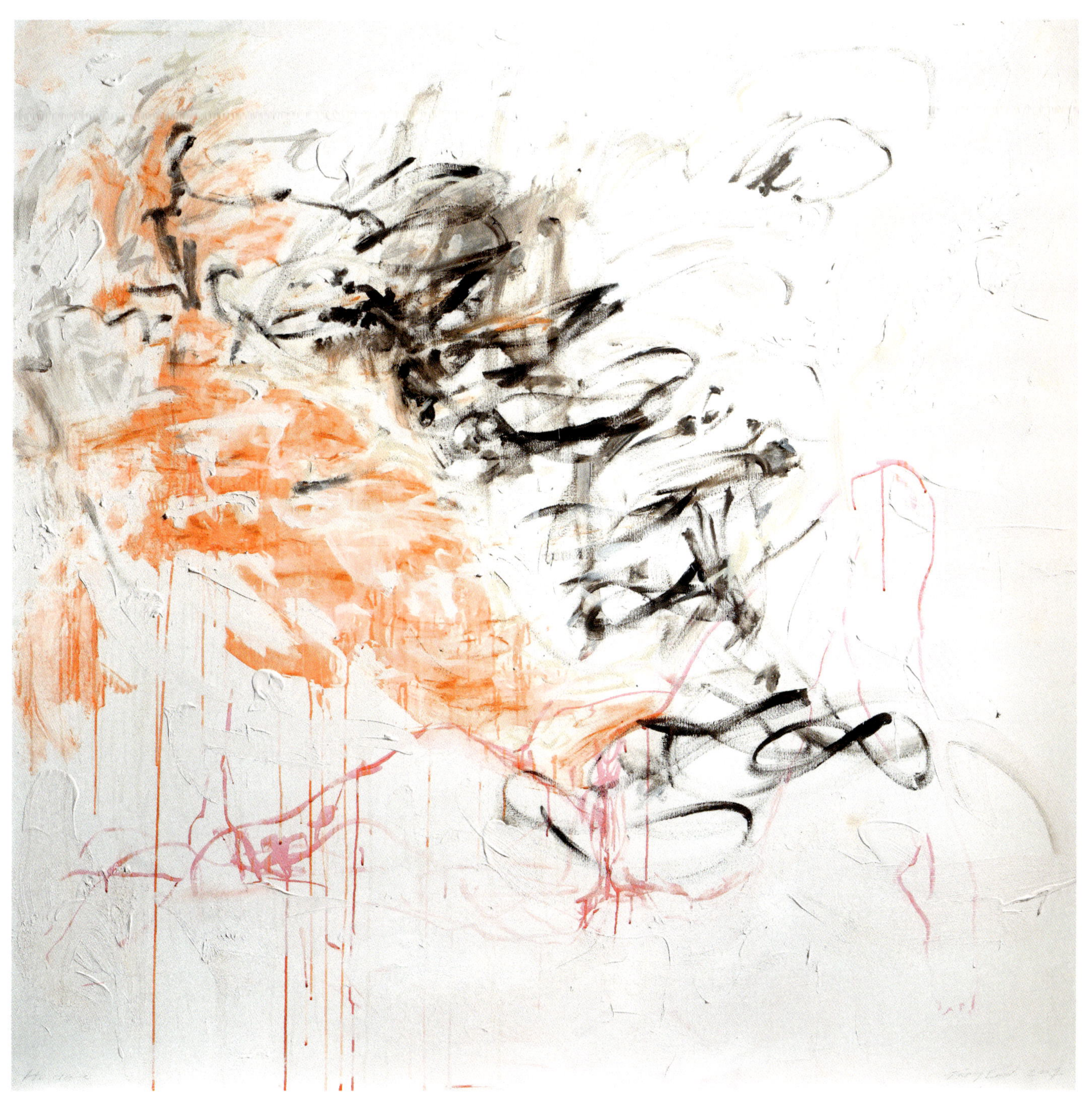

PLATE 1

***Hurricane* 2007**

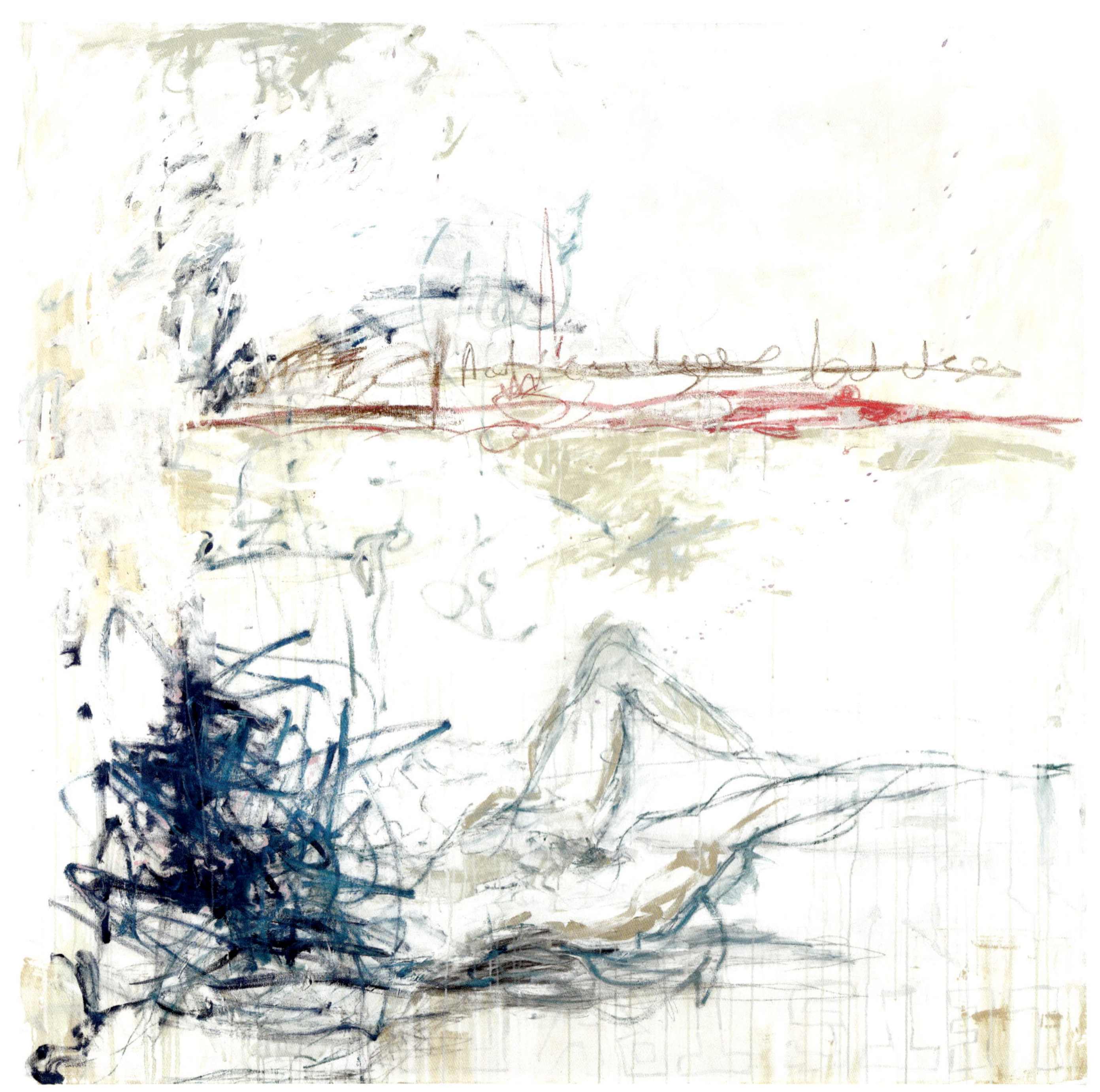

PLATE 2

Pelvis High 2007

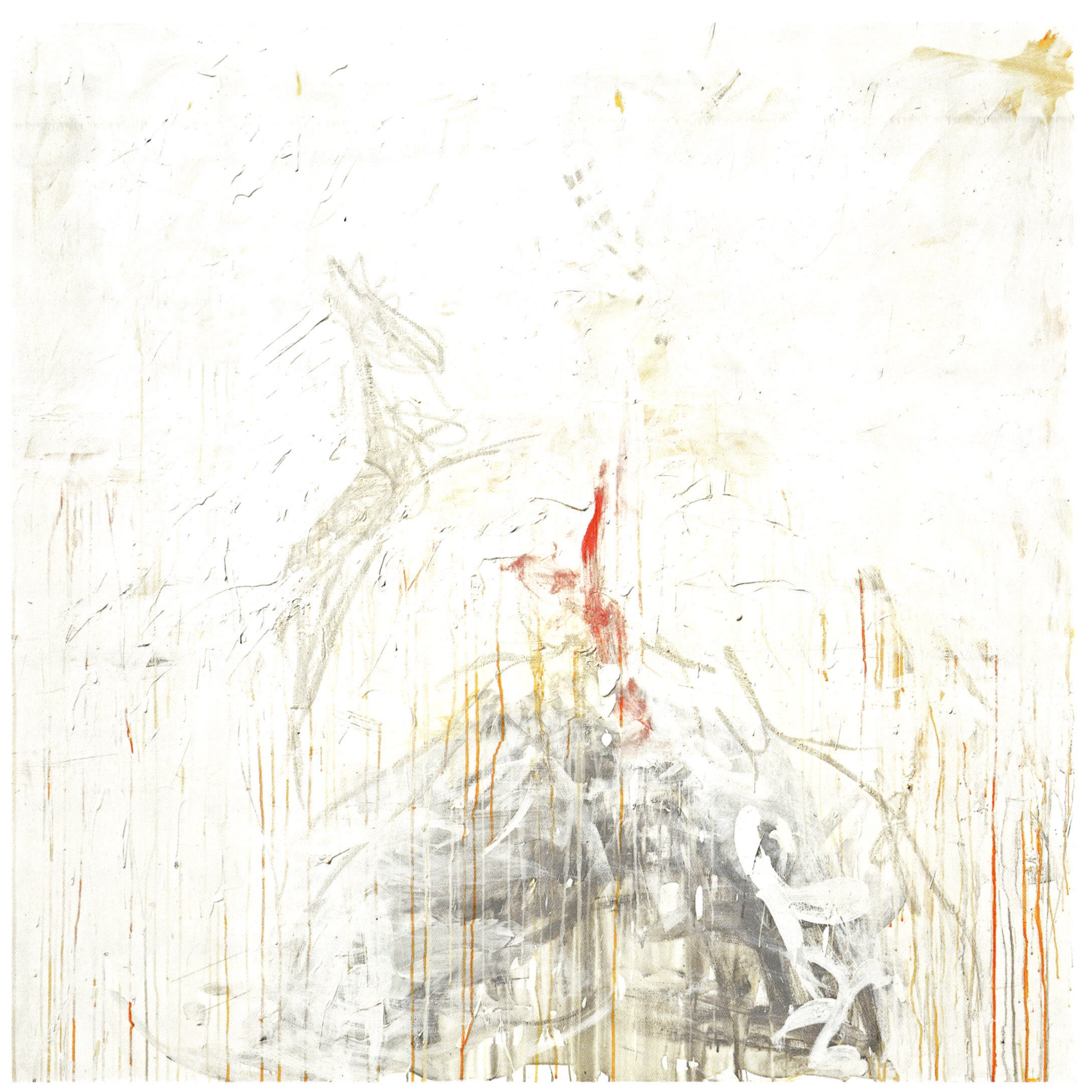

PLATE 3

A rose 2007

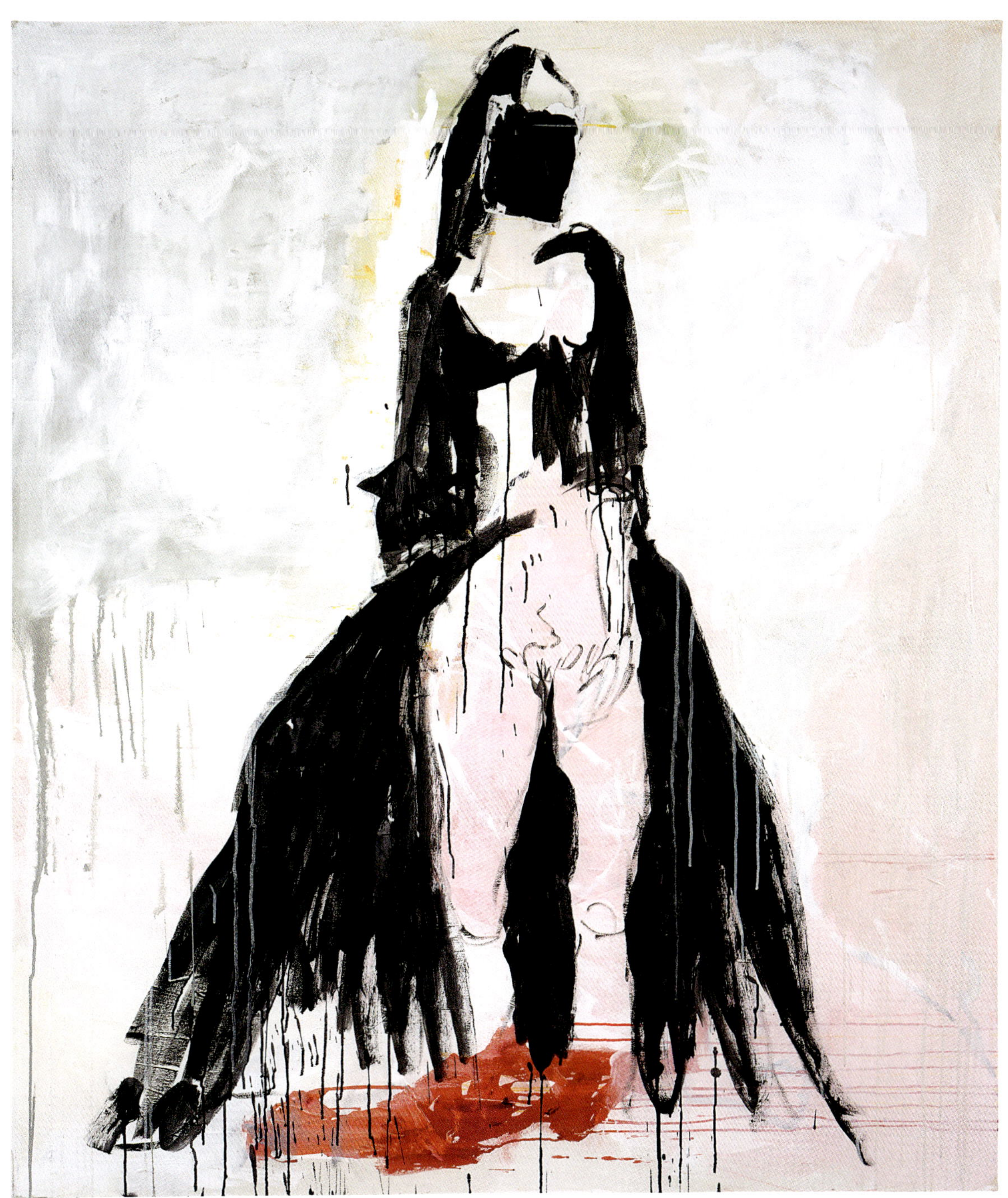

Black Cat 2008

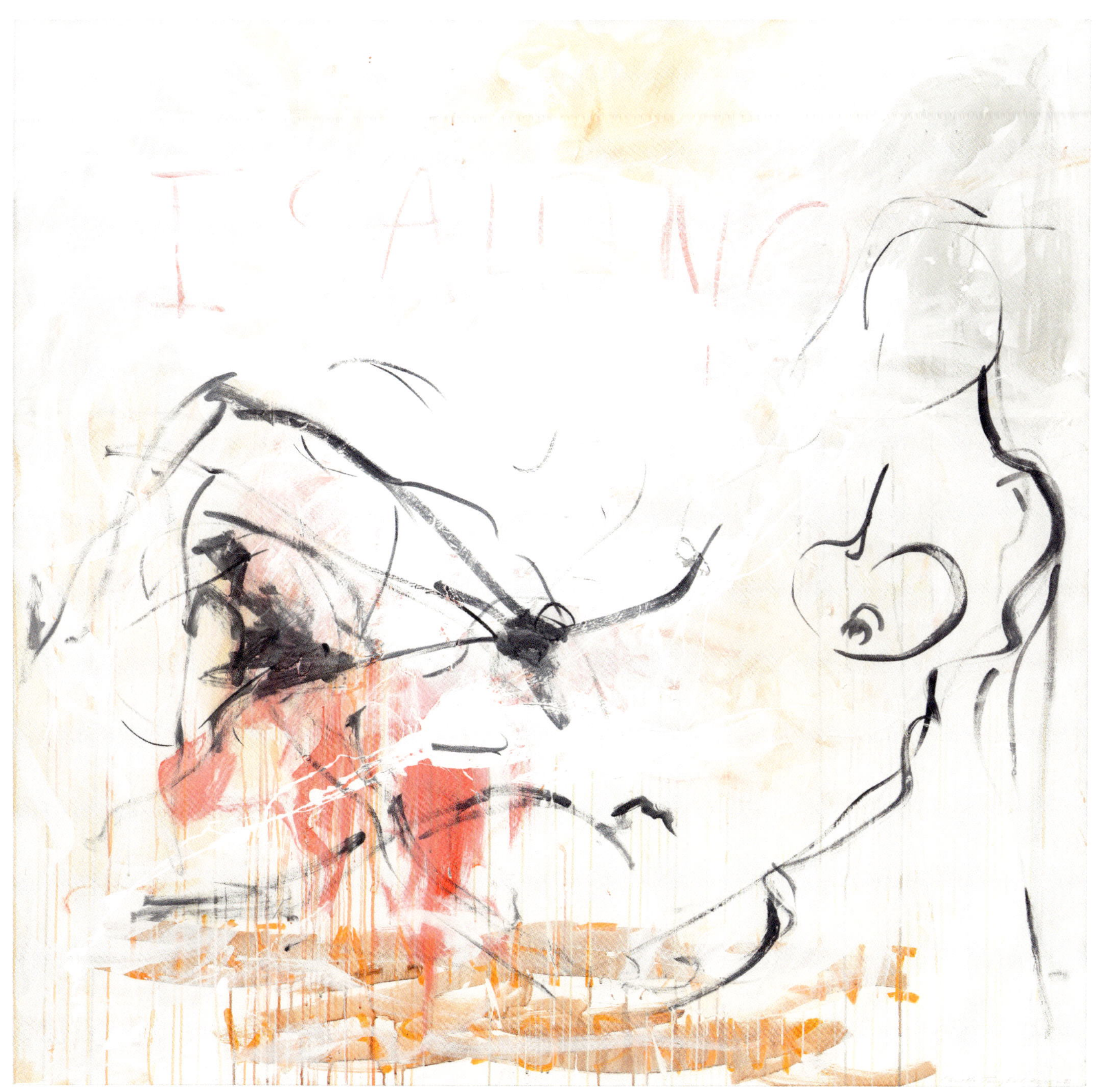

I said No 2005–15

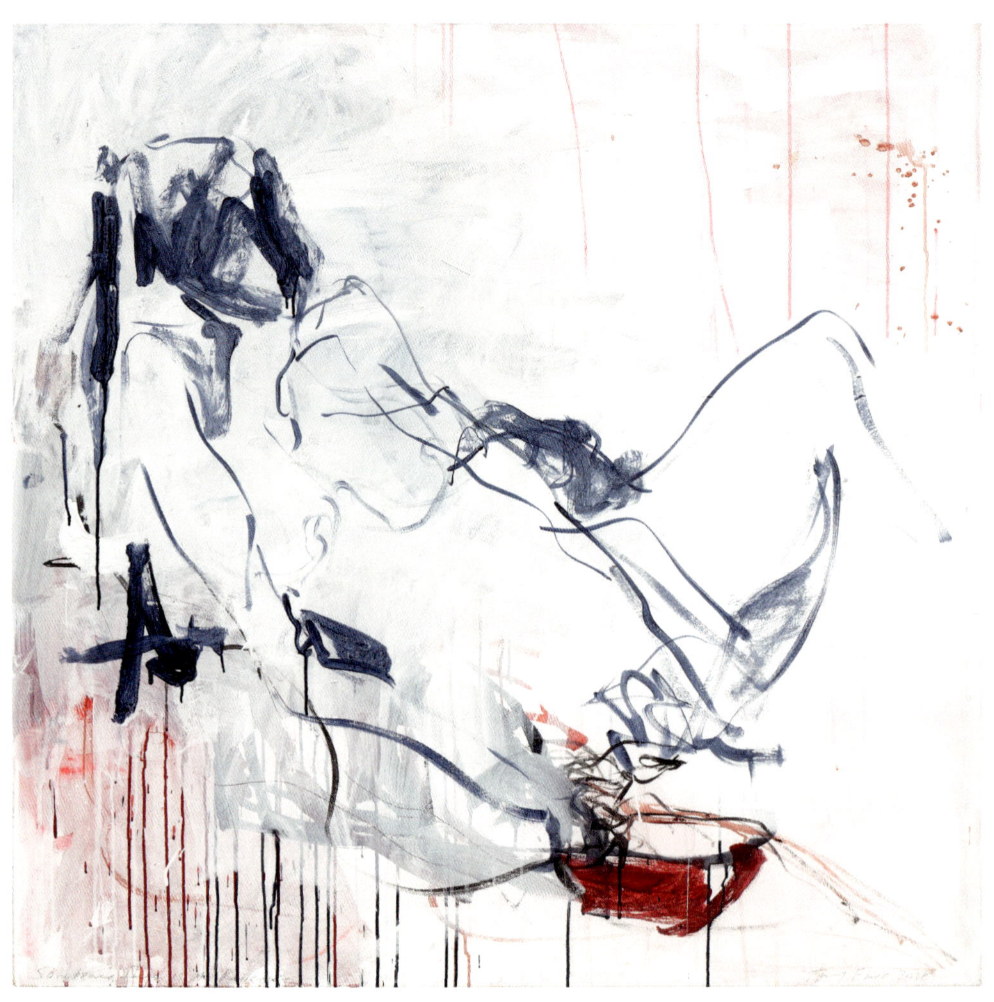

PLATE 6

Sometimes There is No Reason 2018

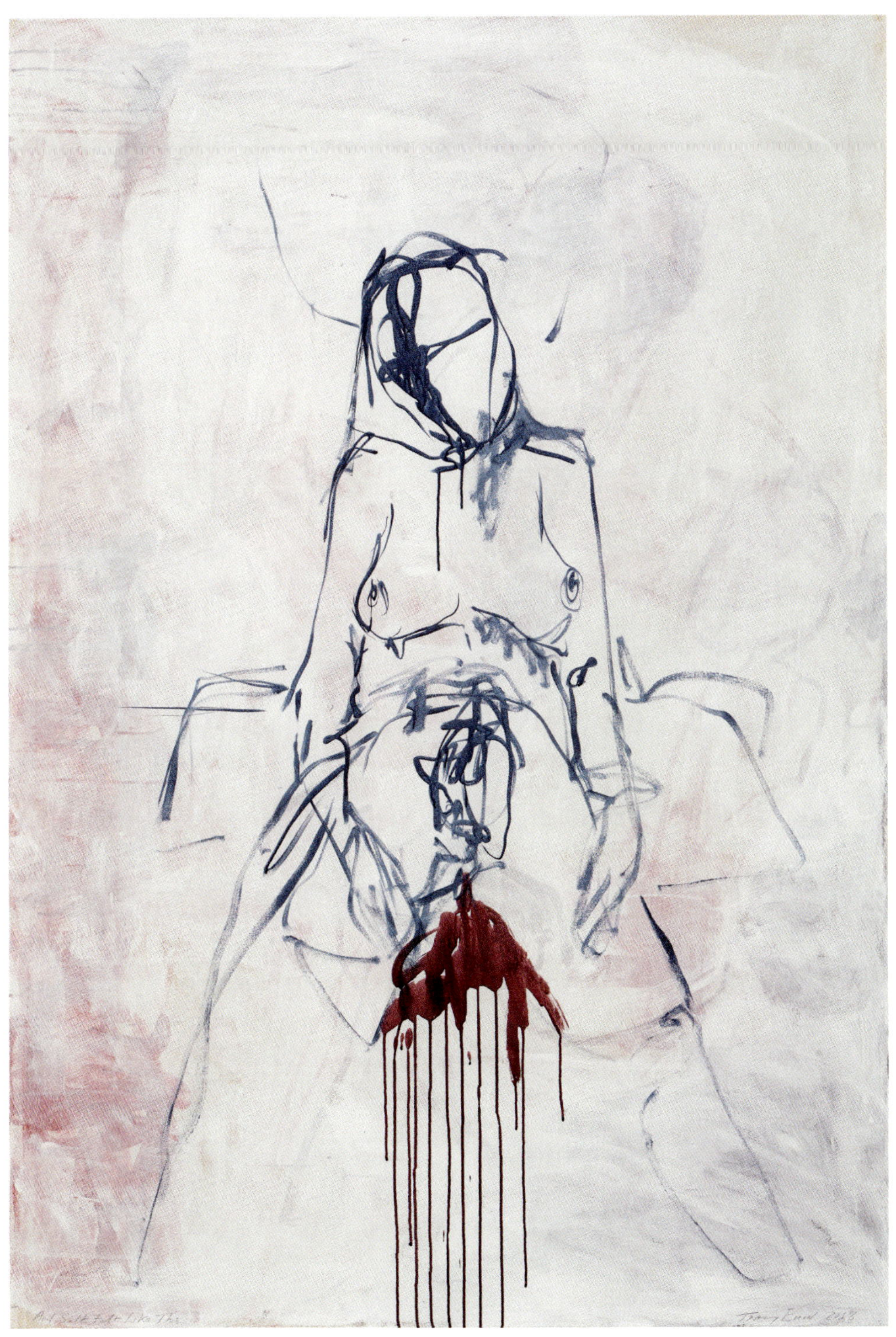

PLATE 7

And So It Felt Like This 2018

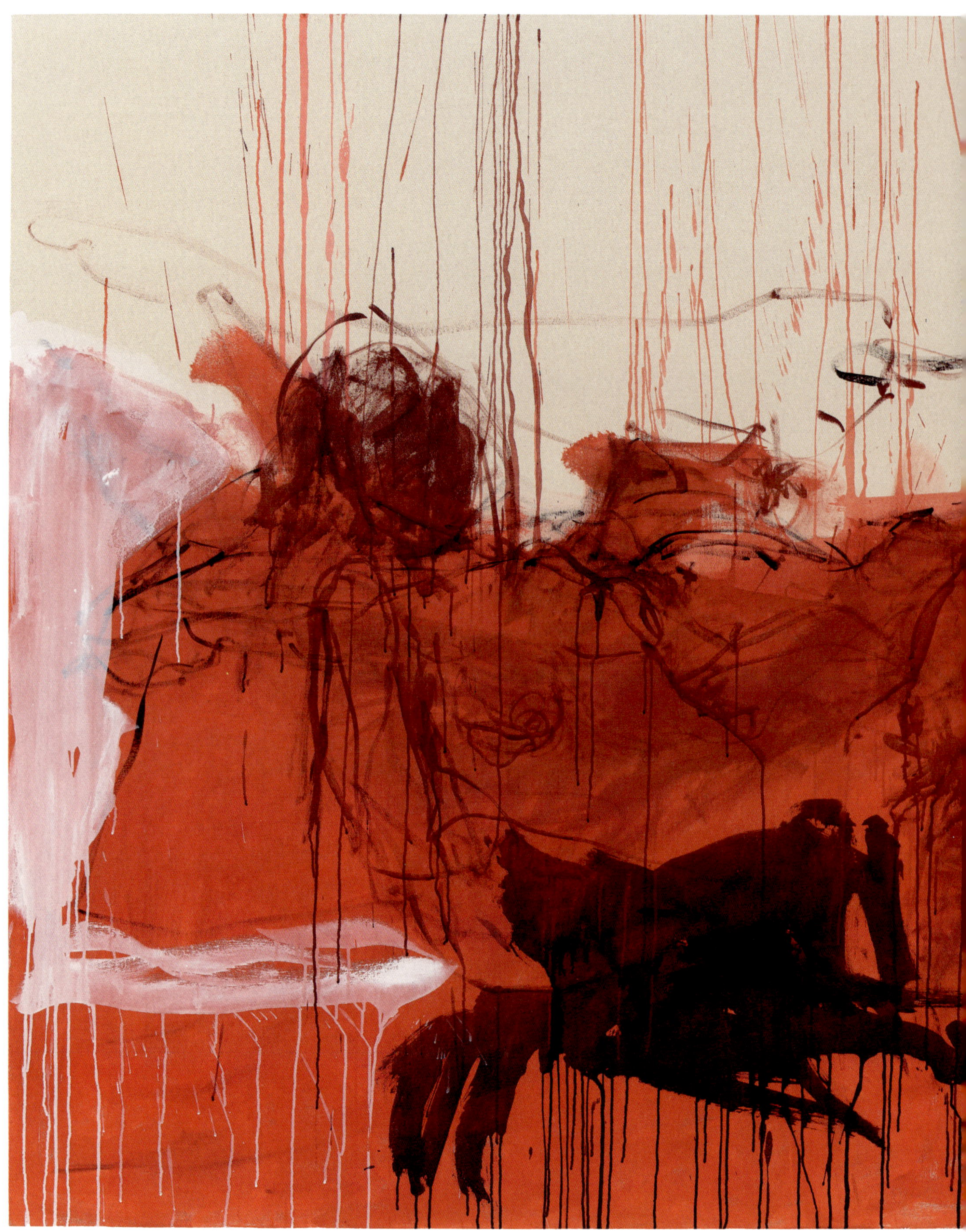

I never Asked to Fall in Love –
You made me Feel like This 2018

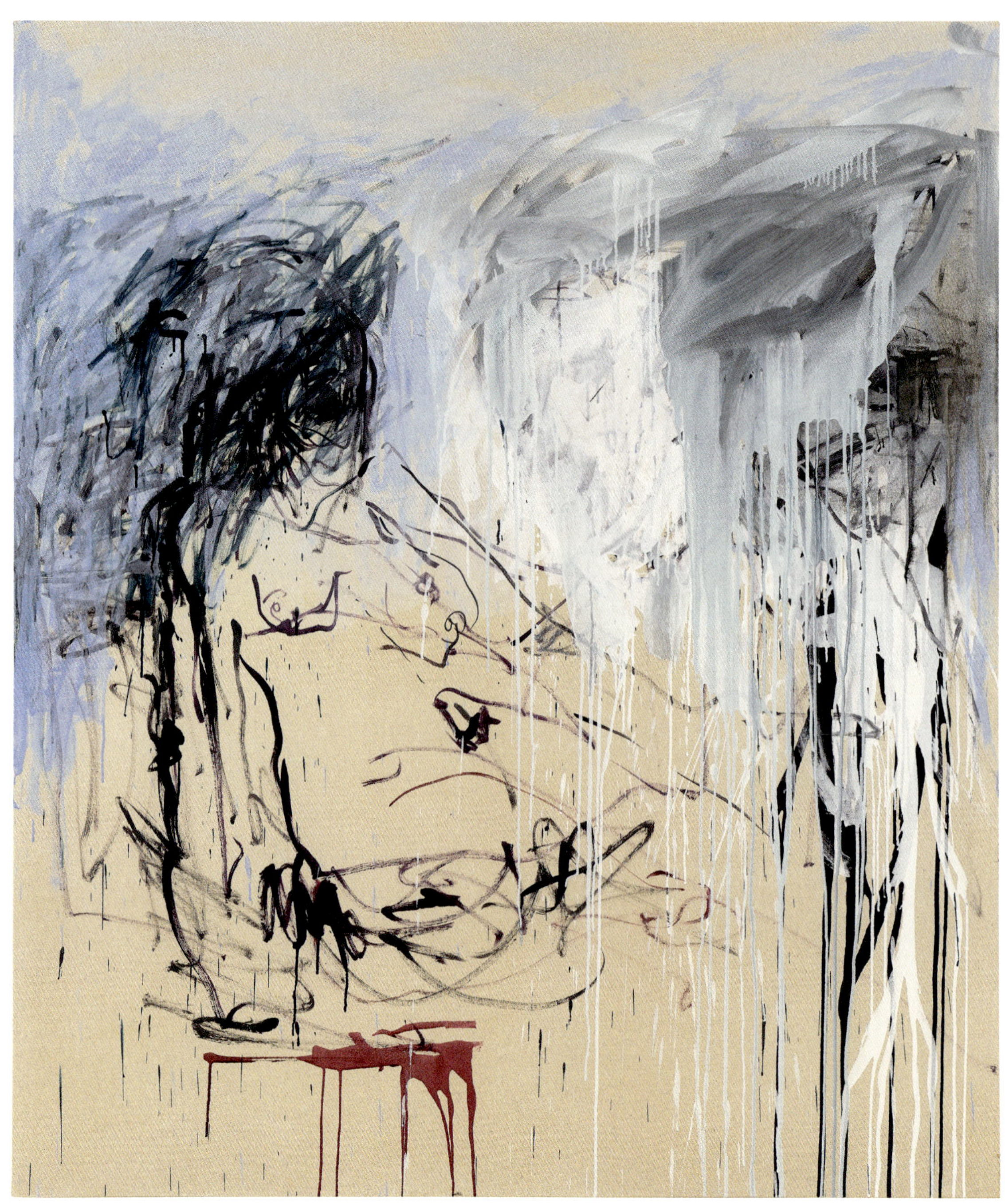

PLATE 9

I wanted you to Fuck The inside of my mind 2018

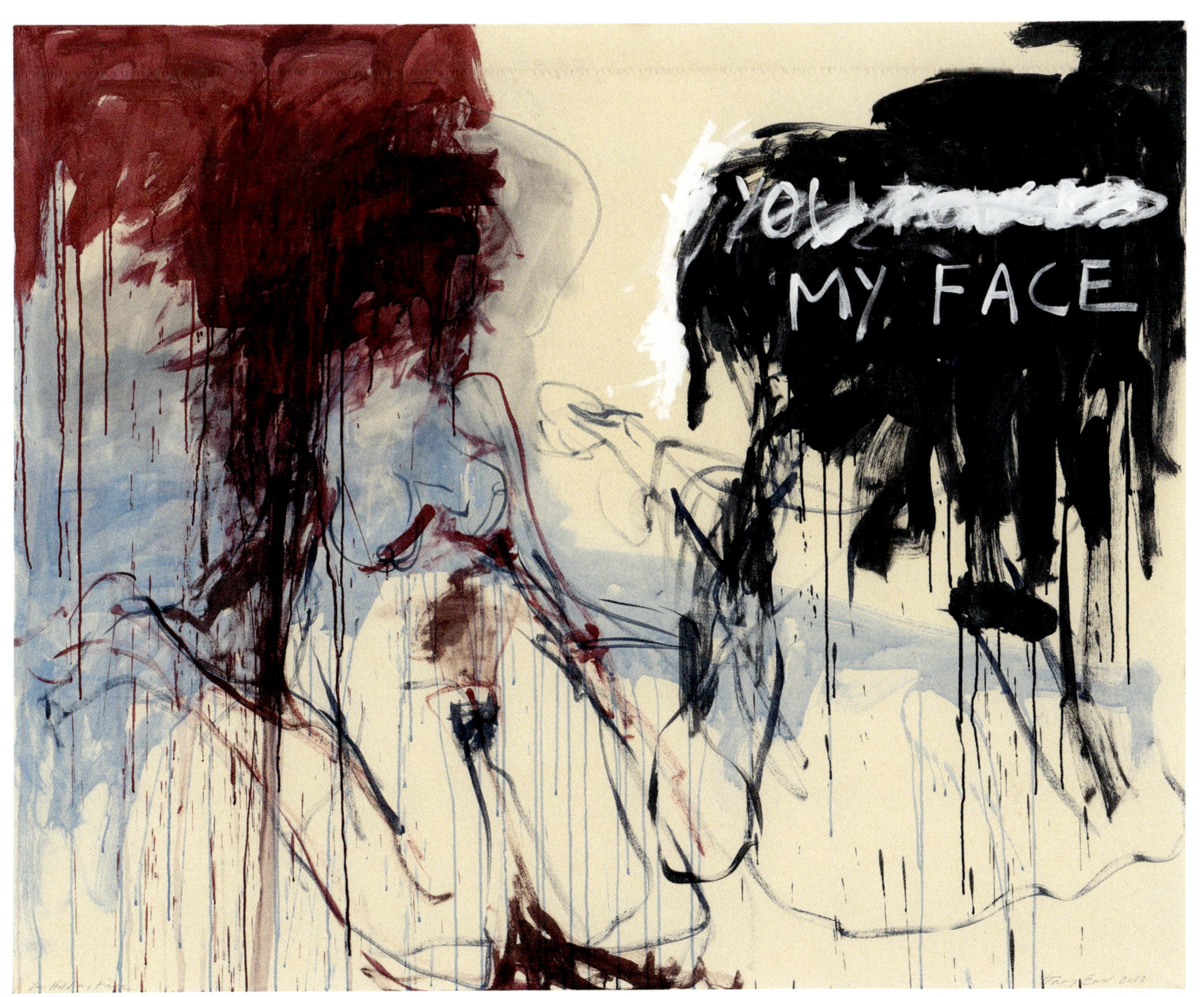

You Held my Face 2018

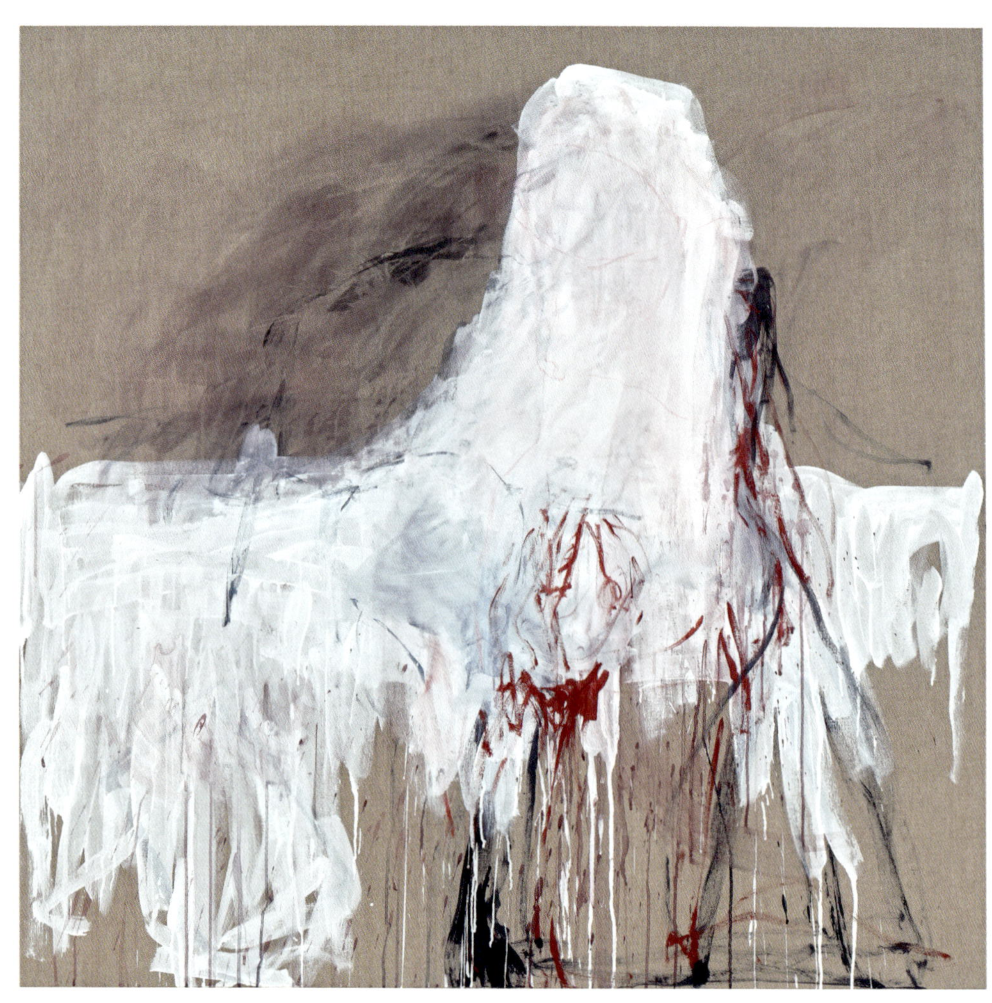

PLATE 11

Ghost of you 2018

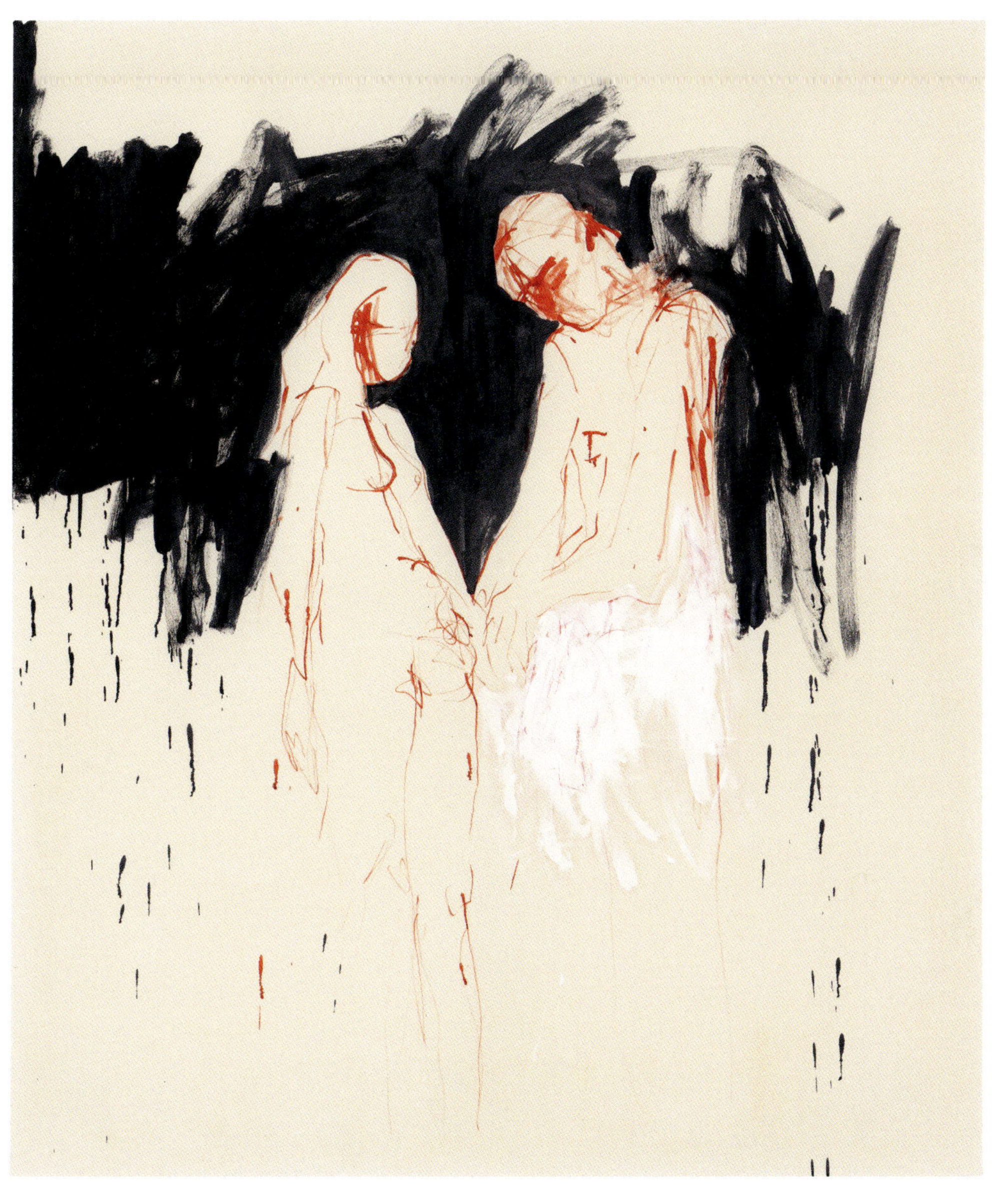

I said I would say goodbye 2019

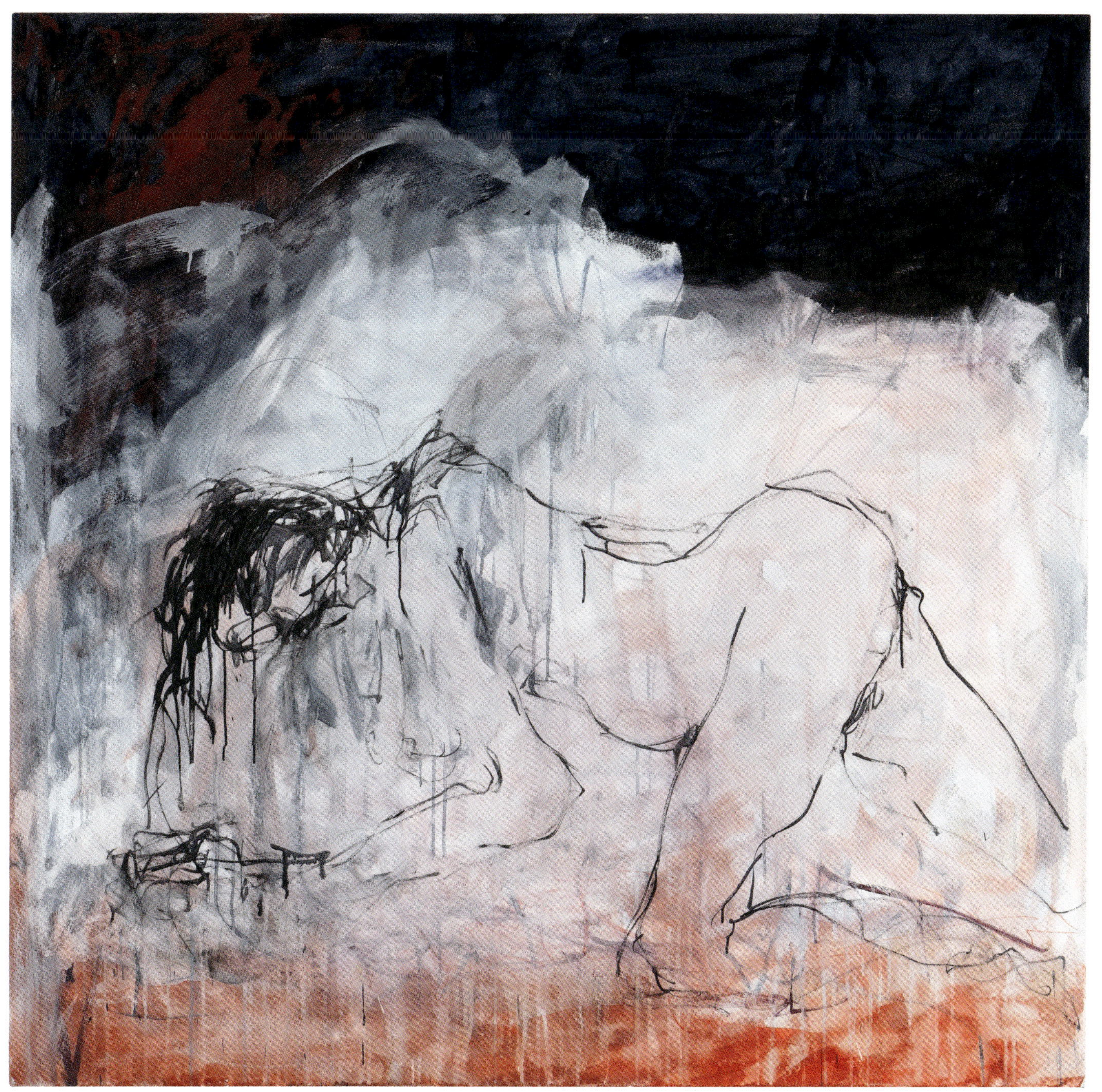

PLATE 13

You kept it coming 2019

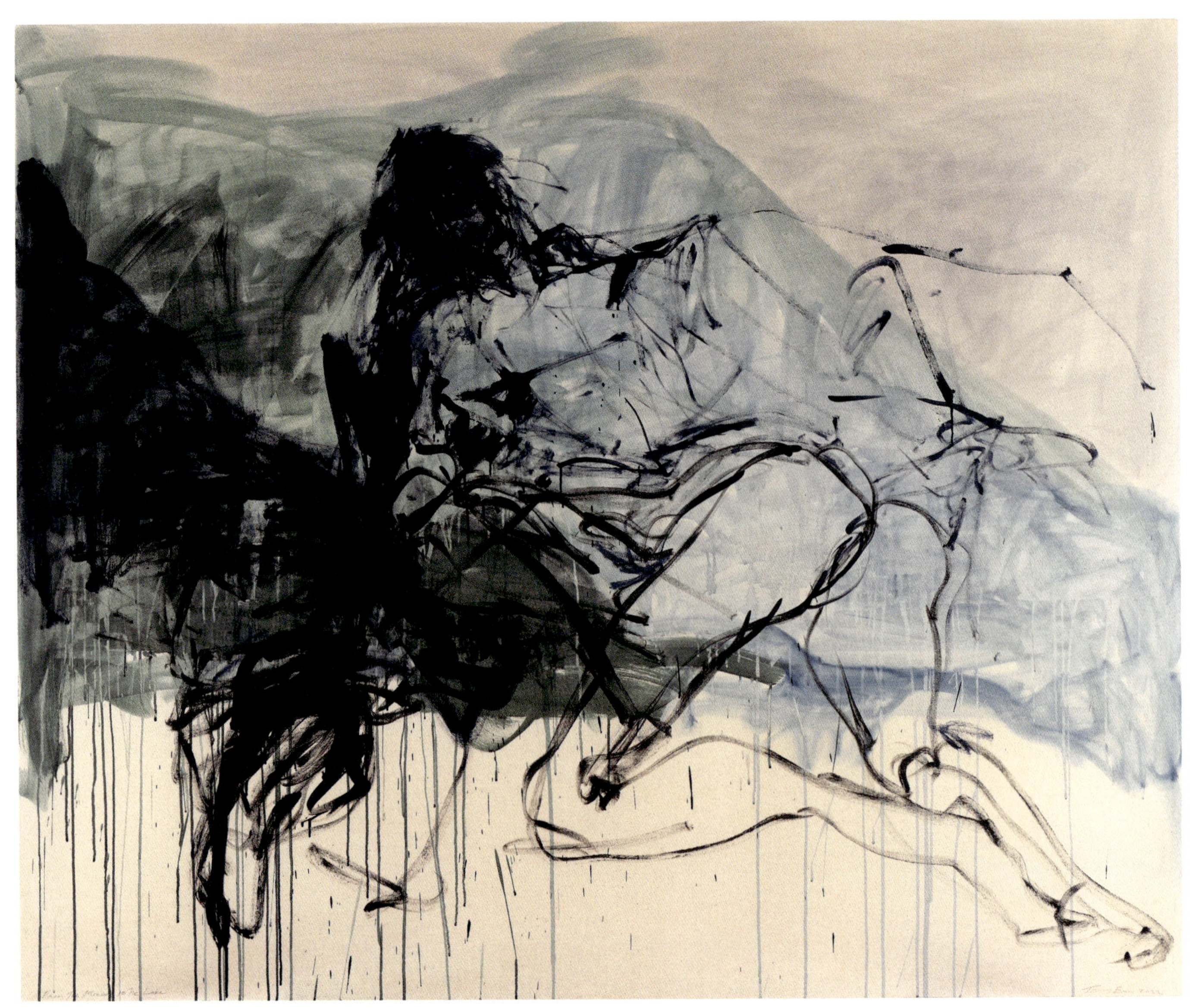

From The Mountain to The Lake 2022

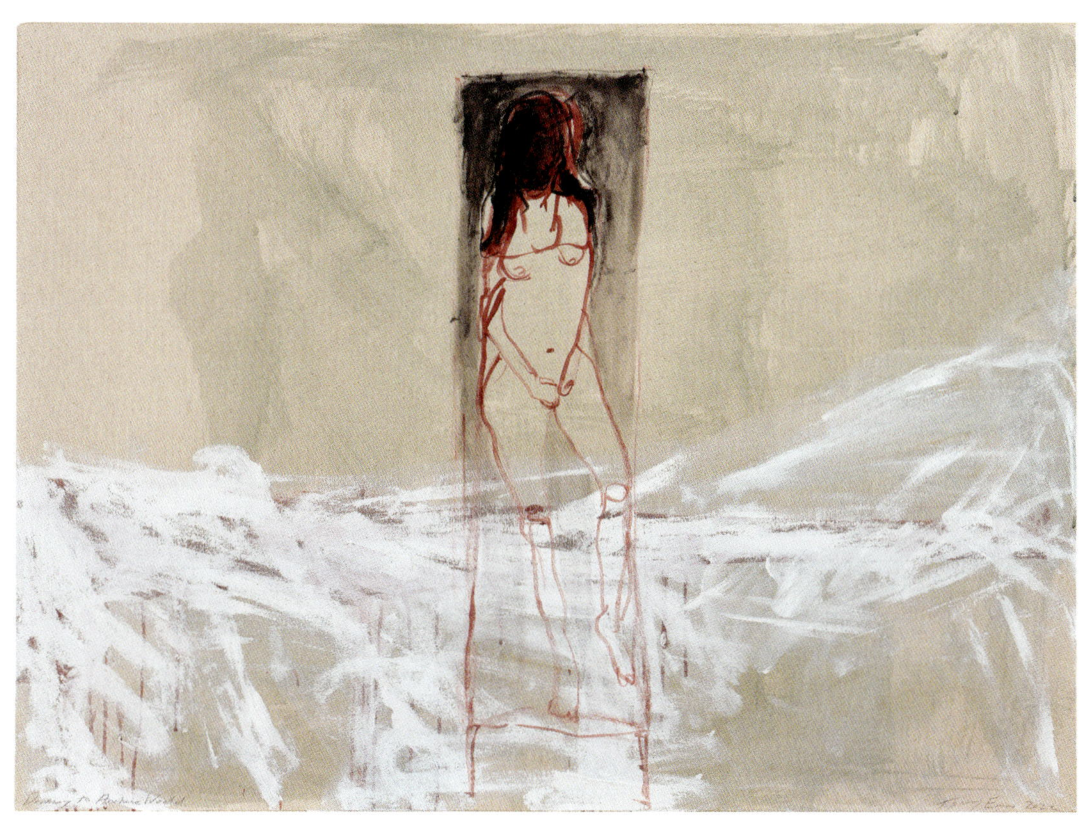

PLATE 15

Dreaming of Another World 2022

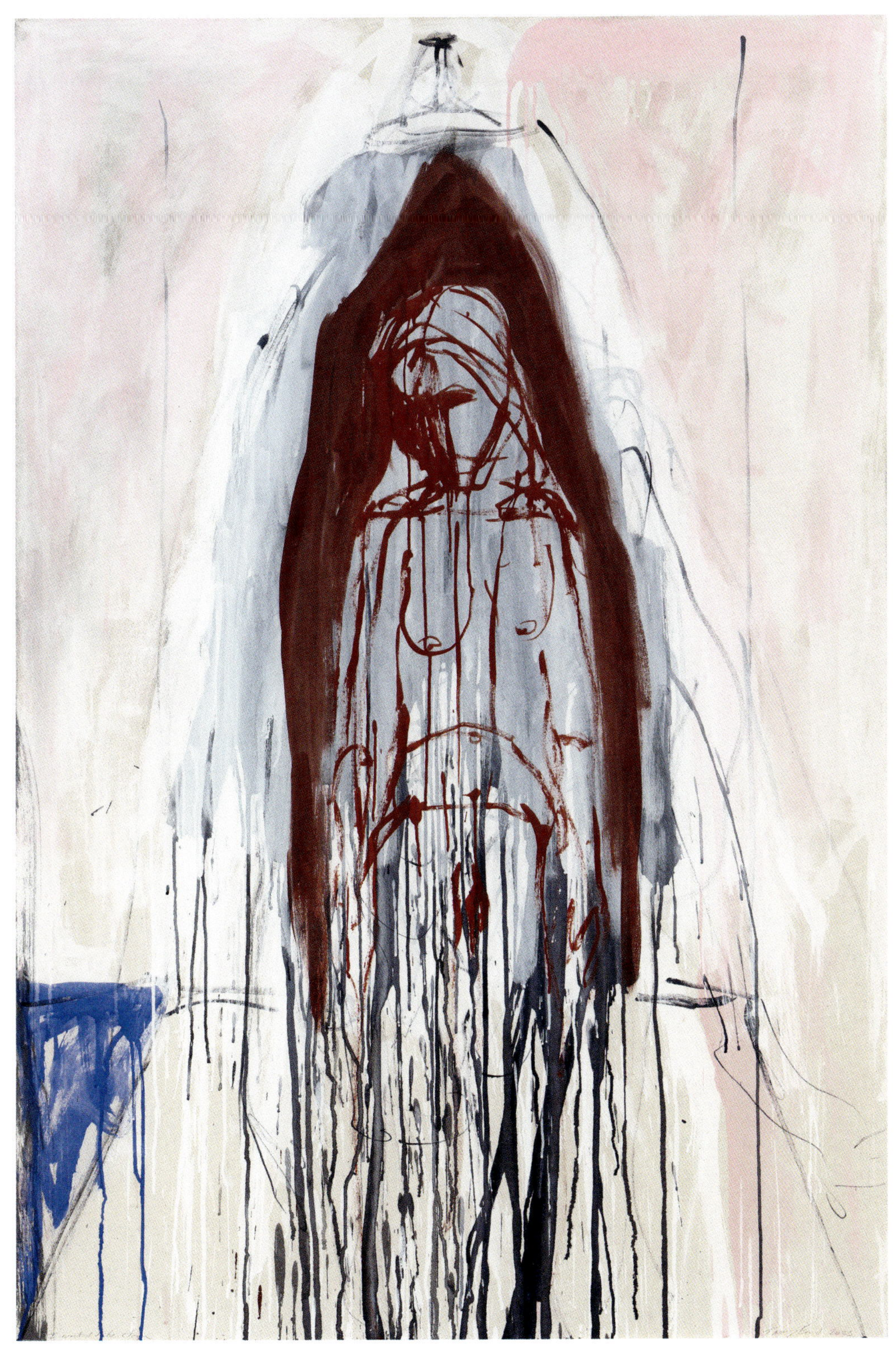

I wanted to be clean 2023

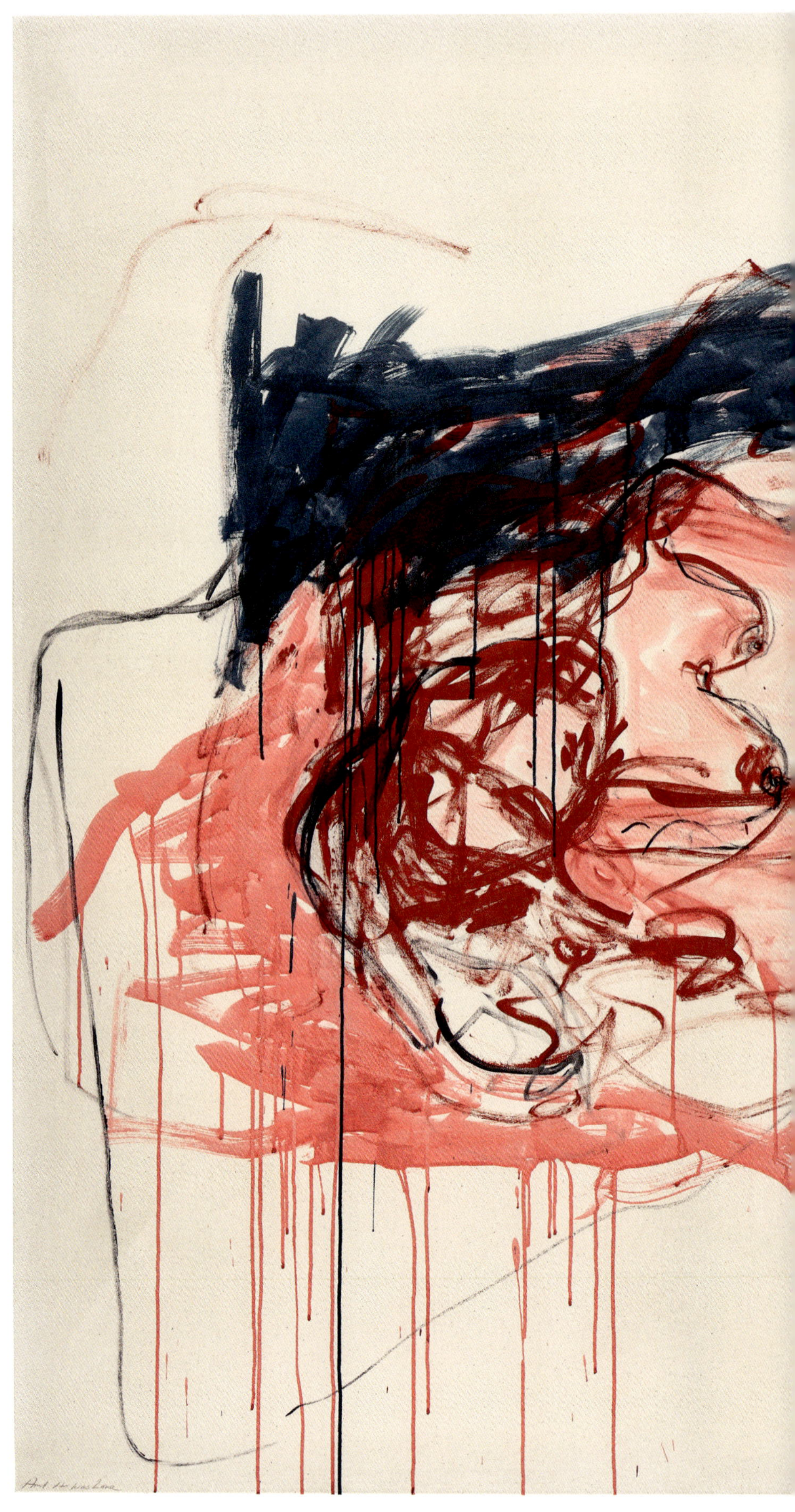

And It was Love 2023

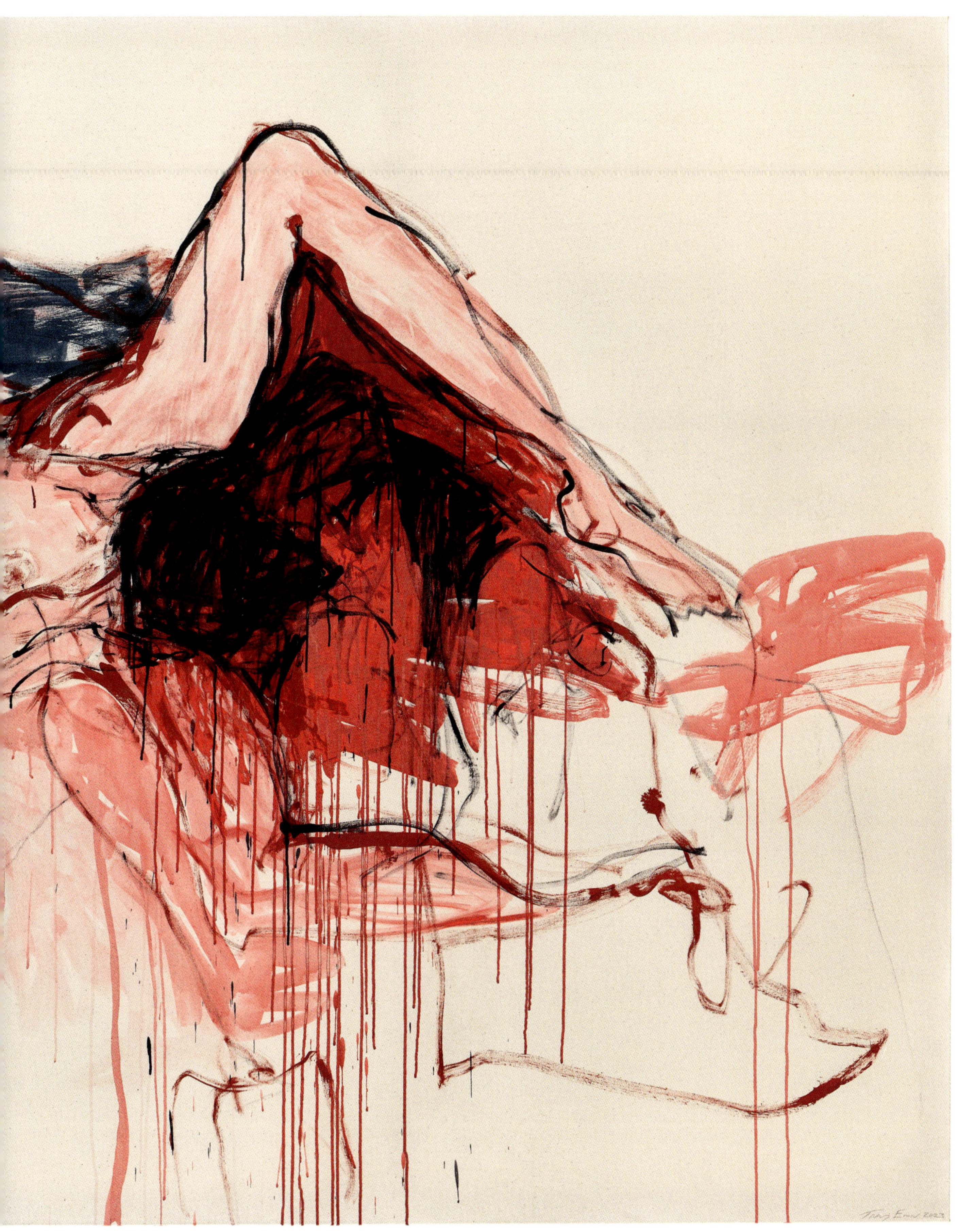

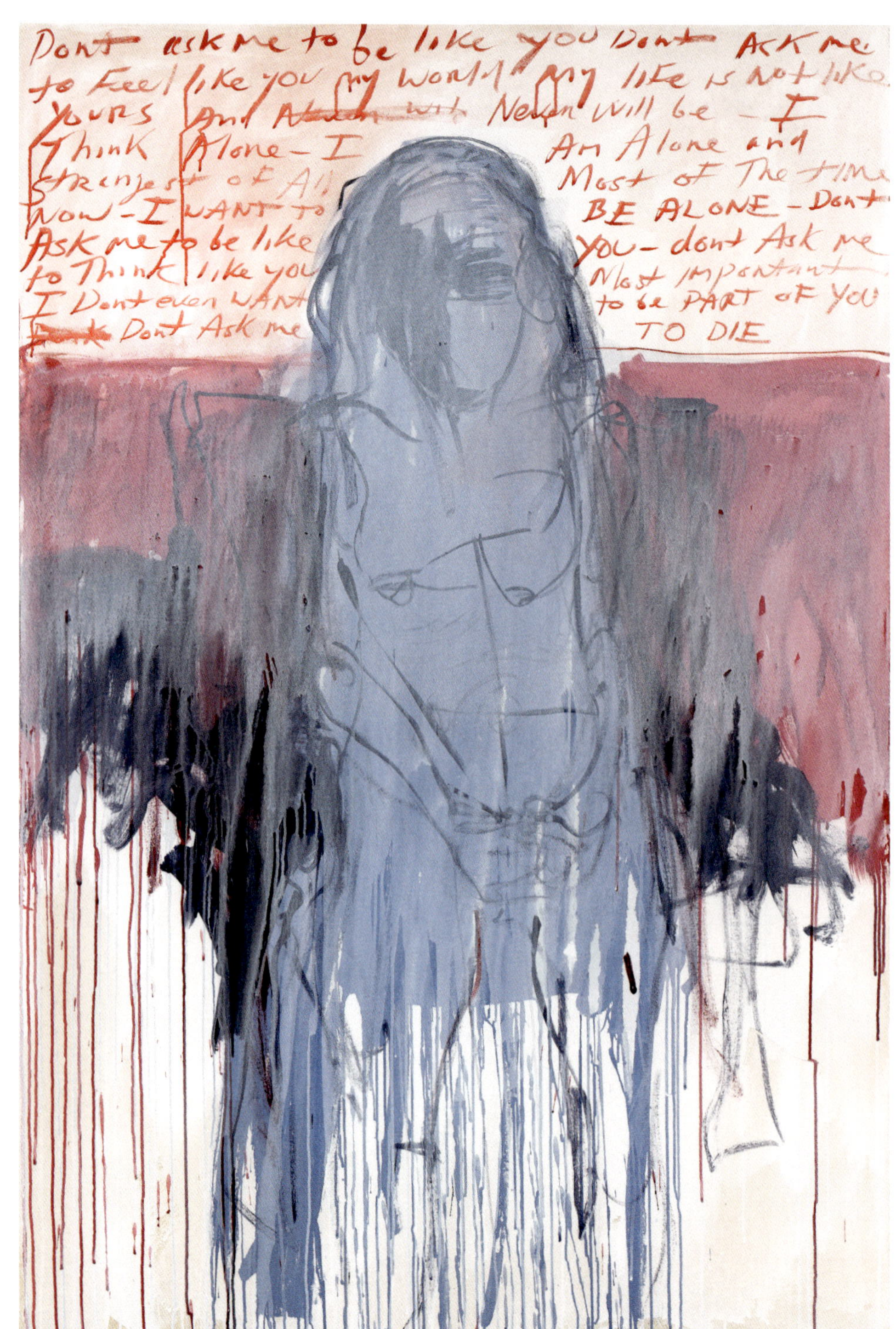

Don't Ask me to be like you 2024

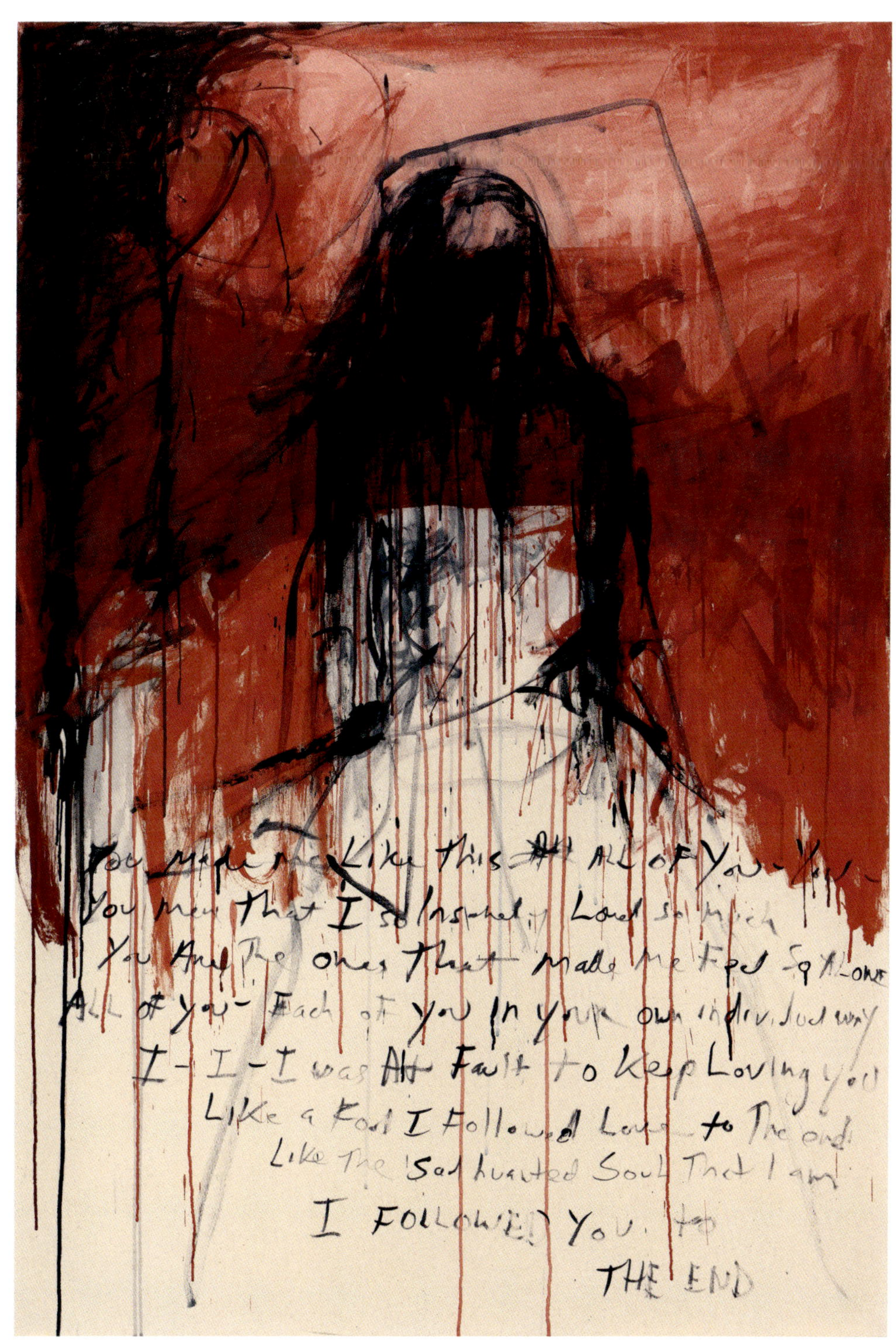

PLATE 19

I Followed you to the end 2024

SCULPTURE

Plates 20–22

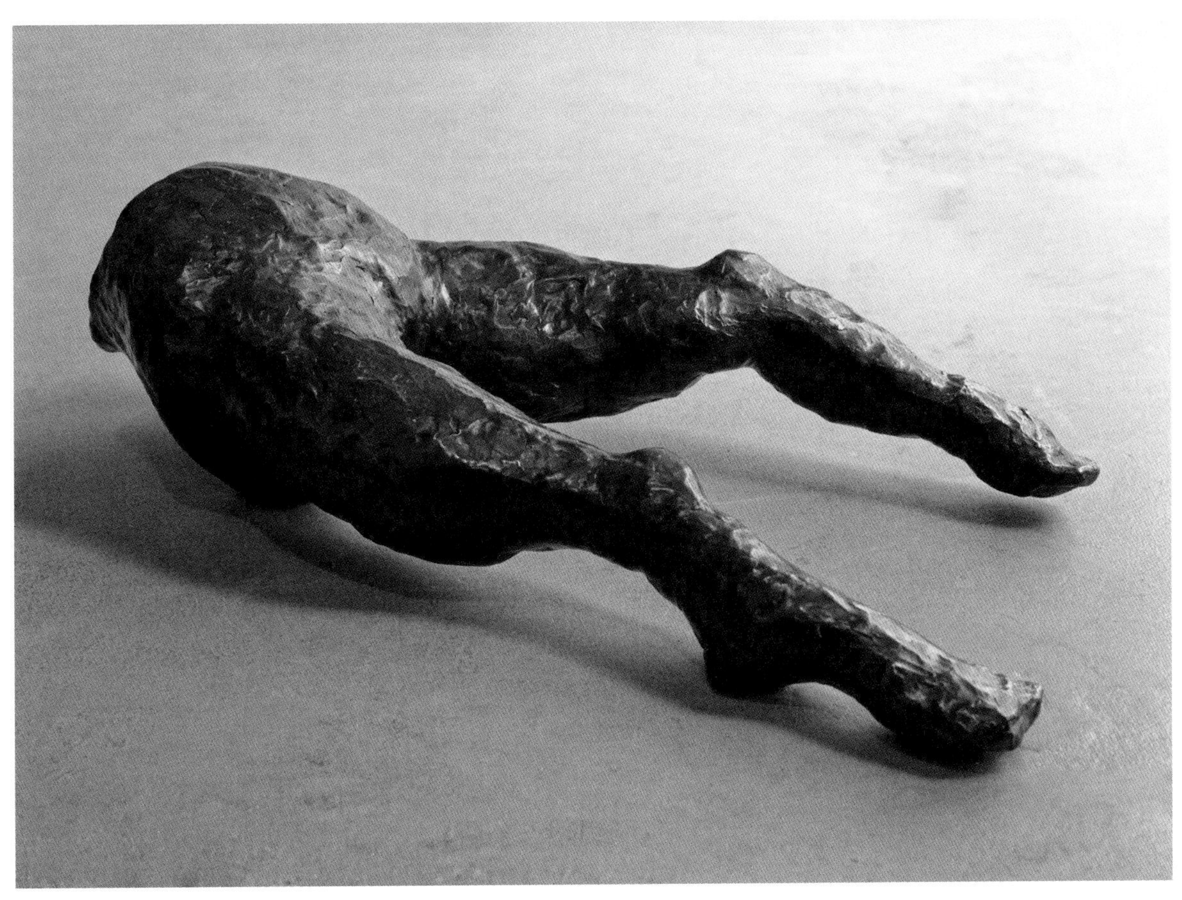

PLATE 20

Without conscience 2014

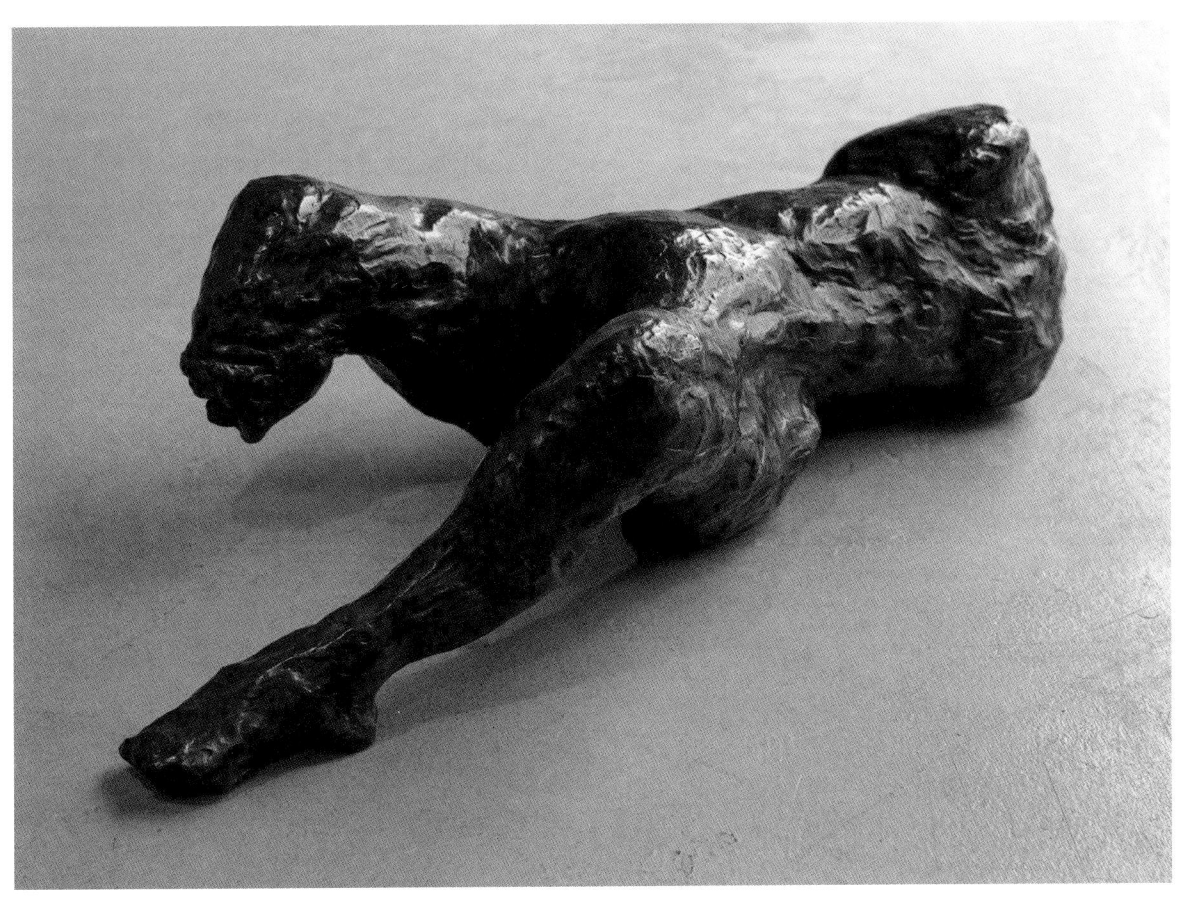

PLATE 21

Every part of me feels you 2014

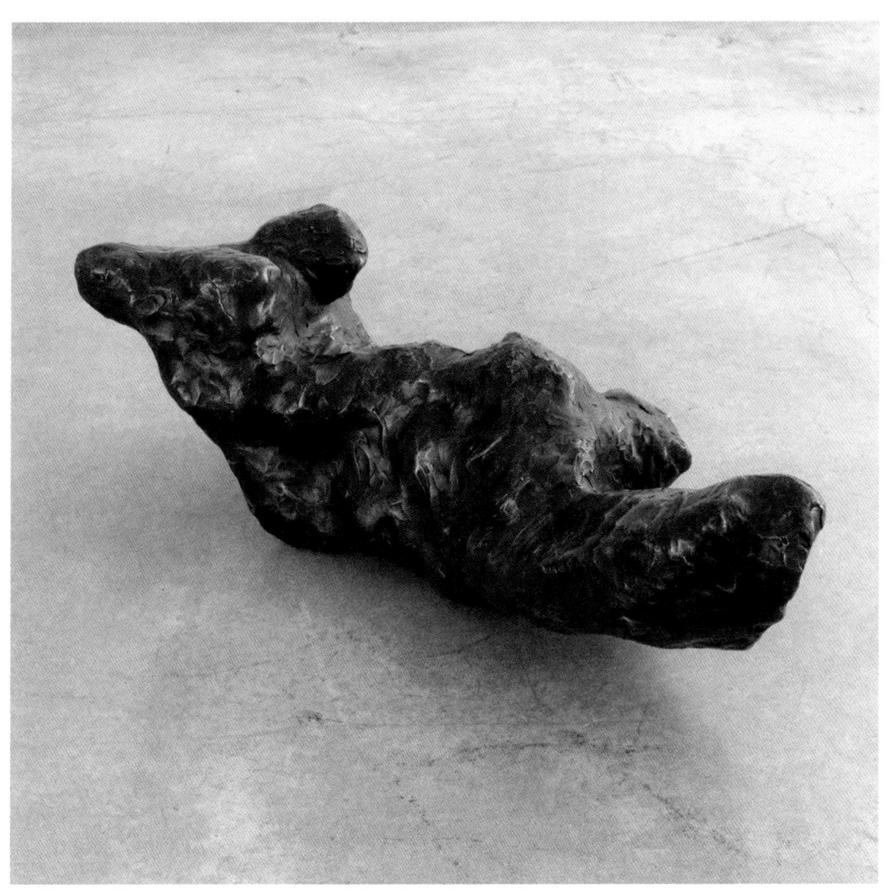

PLATE 22

Landscape 2016

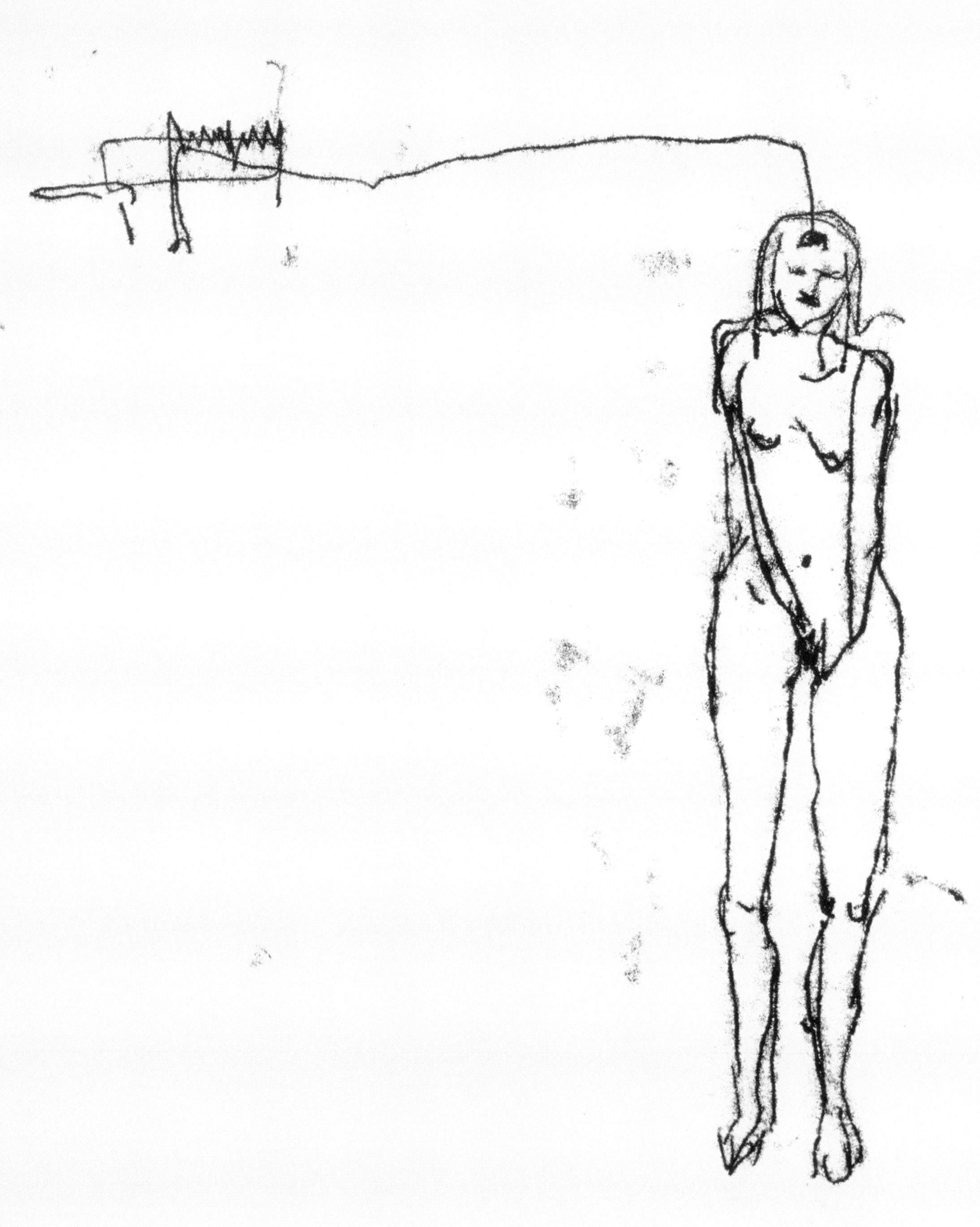

AN ONGOING "BIRTH TO PRESENCE": TRACEY EMIN'S DRAWINGS

Claire Gilman

Tracey Emin recently described the act of drawing as follows: "Drawing is a joining together with mind and hand and heart, a coming together like a unity, like making love. Everything flows and is full. It's a really good feeling. It's about saying, 'here I am,' being present for yourself." Drawing is an expression of intimacy and immediacy as well as a kind of movement or passage: "Work comes from yourself and goes back to yourself," Emin continues. And finally: "Making art is like holding your own hand."[1] Being present, then, is not a condition but a gesture, an act that implies its own dispersal. Consider the 2022 drawing *I Knew you would come* (fig. 1), in which a bird-like figure executed in gray acrylic appears to arrive on the paper as if on a pair of wings, joining a second figure with a mask-like visage. It is hard to say, in fact, if this figure is coming or going, formed as it is by swooping diagonals and stuttering traces. In a related drawing (fig. 2), two prone figures in washy gray hover one above the other. The title, *I left For Ever*, runs along the lower left corner in Emin's familiar slanted hand. Here, the "dream" figure threatens departure while nonetheless clinging insistently to her faceless counterpart beneath, thus belying the drawing's title. In Emin's world there are no absolutes, despite any claim to the contrary.

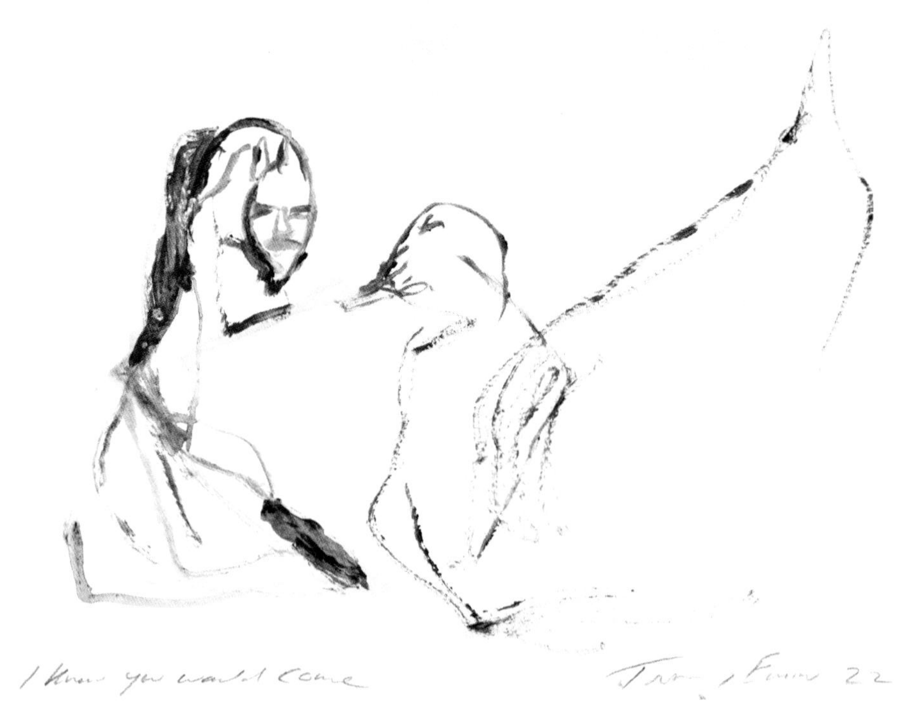

FIG. 1 *I Knew you would come*, 2022. Acrylic on paper, 9 x 12 in. (22.8 x 30.5 cm). Private collection

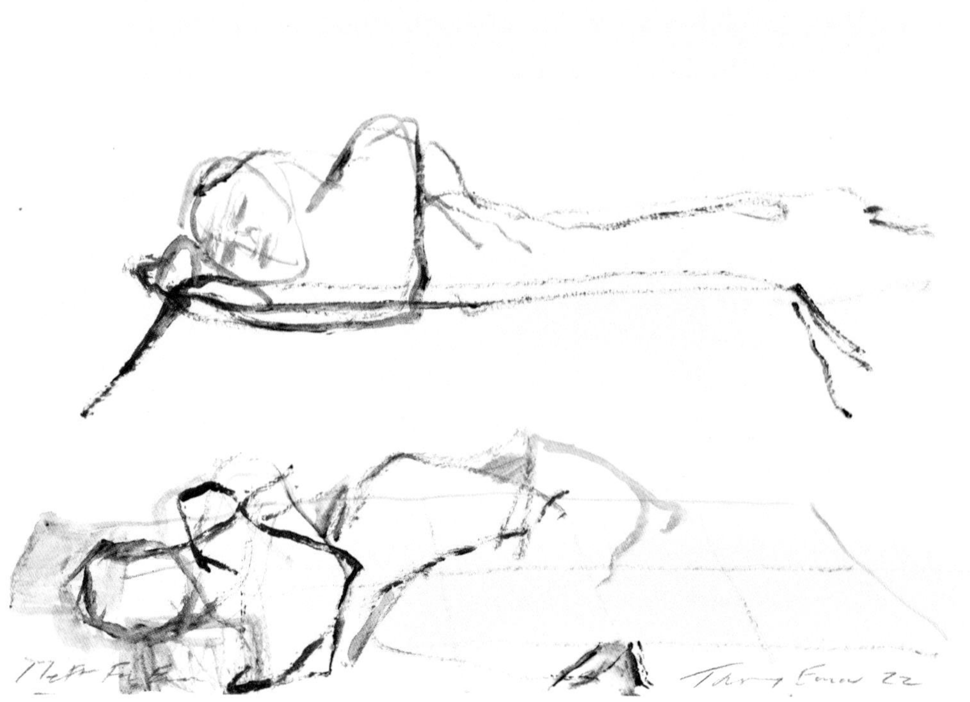

FIG. 2 *I left For Ever*, 2022. Acrylic on paper, 9 x 12 in. (22.8 x 30.5 cm). Private collection

Presence in Emin's work recalls the way in which French philosopher and aesthetician Jean-Luc Nancy defines it in his 1993 collection of essays *The Birth to Presence*, wherein presence is understood as "a *coming*," as "what is born, and does not cease being born. Of it and to it there is birth, and only birth.... Not form and fundament, but the pace, the passage, the coming in which nothing is distinguished, and everything is unbound."[2] For Nancy, things are never self-contained. Rather, there is the "infinitely intimate stirring of the thing in itself, on itself, this repetition of the thing itself... whose meaning starts to tremble." How, he asks, does a thing come to exist as the thing that it is, "not a form cut out of matter, nor a material that fills a form, but this rising, this lifting — the plasticity."[3]

It is this rising and lifting that we witness in *I Knew you would come* and *I left For Ever* and that Emin herself consistently invokes when describing her approach to artmaking and life in general. I "think with my body like a bird"; "I want my mind to float into another's"; "I dream of living somewhere with space" are some of her many declarations on the subject in her 2005 memoir *Strangeland*.[4] In the wake of her 2020 cancer diagnosis, she describes her new approach to life and its eventual termination as an act of transit: "I'm building my journey to death. I'm building my way forward."[5] Drawing for Emin is similarly processual. It involves "pull[ing]" events to the front of her mind and "forc[ing] the drawing out of my hand.... I am the custodian, the curator, of the images that live in my mind," and that pass from it onto the paper.[6]

Emin has observed a change in her work in recent years coinciding with her acceptance of mortality and aging, one that she explains resulted in an entirely different way of approaching the drawn medium. For years, her primary drawings were monotypes made by applying ink to glass and yielding fragile images of largely solitary figures on otherwise empty pages. One day, she said, she turned instead to direct representations in ink and watercolor in loose, fluid strokes.

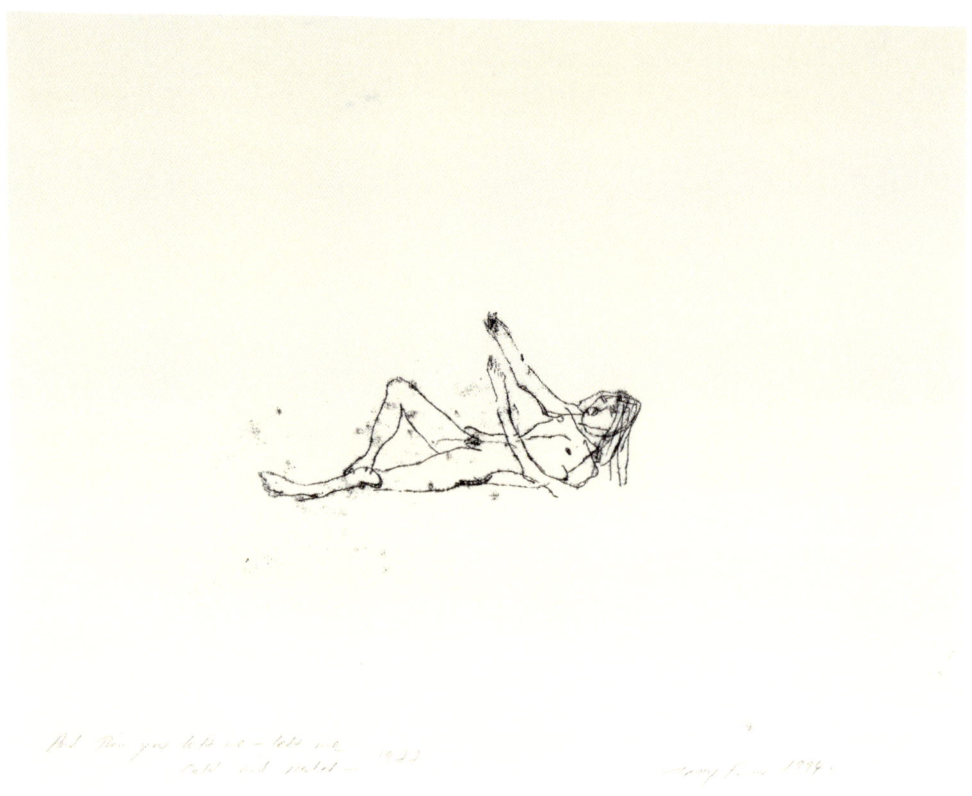

FIG. 3 *And Then you left me – left me cold and naked – 1977*, 1994. Monoprint, 16⅜ x 20¼ in. (41.5 x 51.3 cm). British Museum, London

These new drawings, as she put it, were more like making love, while the others were like masturbation — something inward and private and alone. In her words: "one is wet and the other is dry; one is fluid and the other is rigid; one voluptuous and open and the other stiff; one full and the other shaky."[7] Where the monotypes contract, the later drawings fill up space. Notably, the difference lies less in Emin's subject matter — love, sex, trauma, and loss remain her consistent themes — than in her approach, as though it is her perspective on her subjects, rather than the themes themselves, that has changed.

This difference is starkly evident when comparing two images made thirty years apart: the monotype *And Then you left me — left me cold and naked — 1977* (fig. 3) from 1994, and *I Felt Bereft — How could you do this to me* (fig. 4), a drawing in acrylic on paper from 2023. In both compositions, a woman lies prone in an otherwise empty space, her head raised as she gazes out in supplication. But

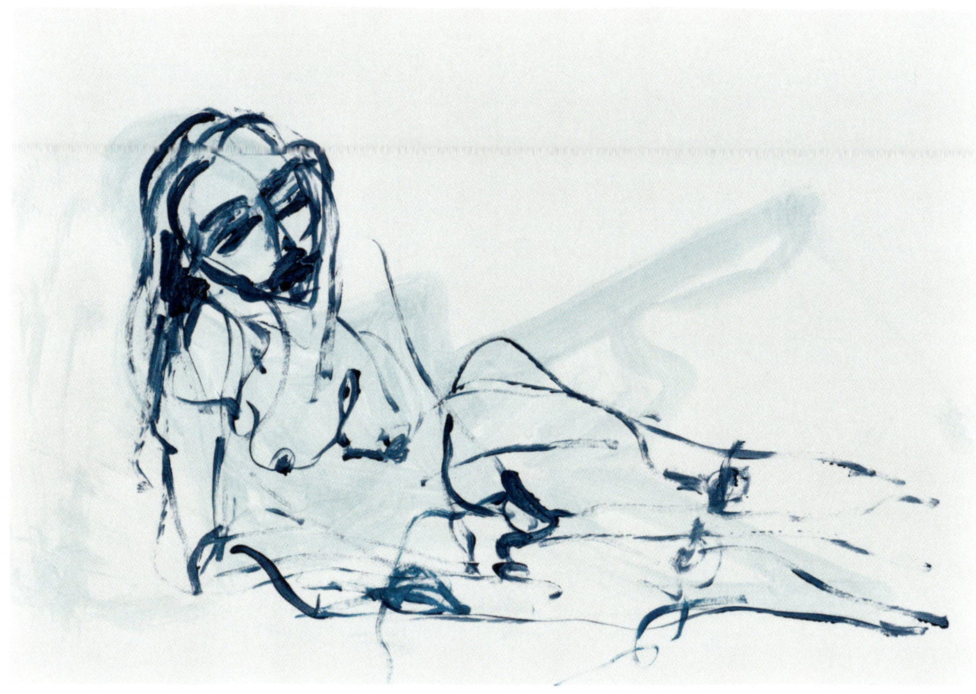

here the similarities end. In the earlier image, the figure is small and fragile in her vast expanse, executed in the jittery black line characteristic of the monotypes. In the later work, the figure is large and weighty, filling the page with saturated blue lines that overflow the body's contour and seep into the white ground. This woman is bereft but in control, momentarily anchored by her supporting arm, whereas the girl in the monotype is precariously unstable; arms outstretched, she will not be able to sustain her position for long. In this sense, despite its painful subject, the 2023 drawing shares more in common with the 2020 image *Filling up the empty room* (fig. 5), in which Emin's solitary figure is now seen confidently stretched out on a chaise lounge. Her black contour lines extend into the blue lines that define the couch and the rug beneath, her pink skin of the same stuff and substance as the pink of the couch and the wall behind it. She is an integral part of her surroundings.

And yet, what is crucial here — and what remains consistent throughout Emin's work — is the sense of movement that pervades the composition. This

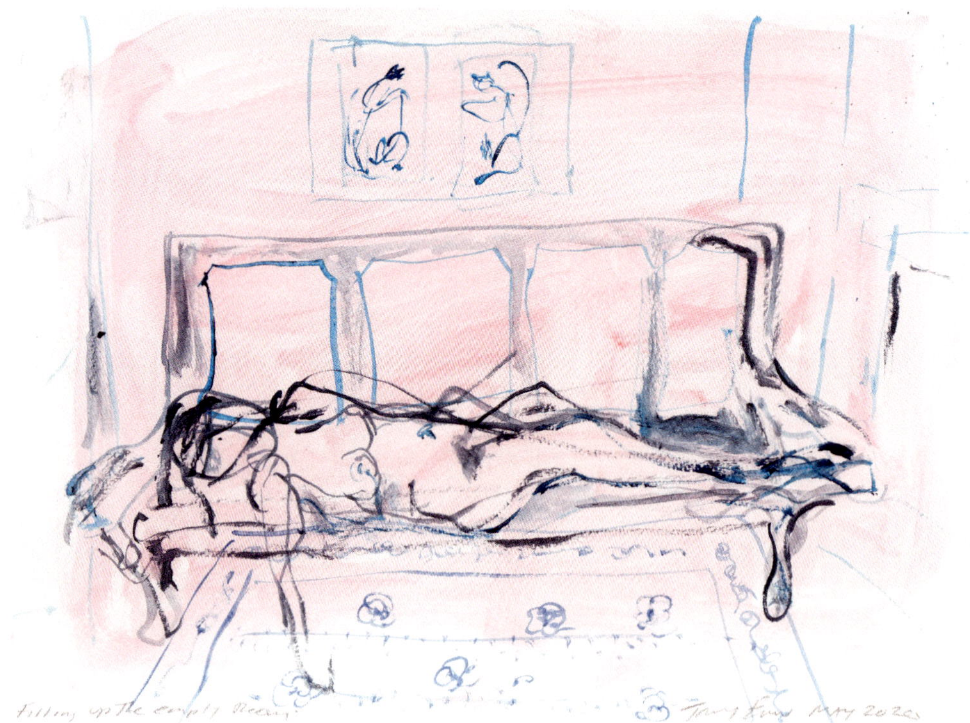

FIG. 5 *Filling up The empty Room*, 2020. Gouache on paper, 9⅜ x 12½ in. (23.9 x 31.9 cm). Private collection

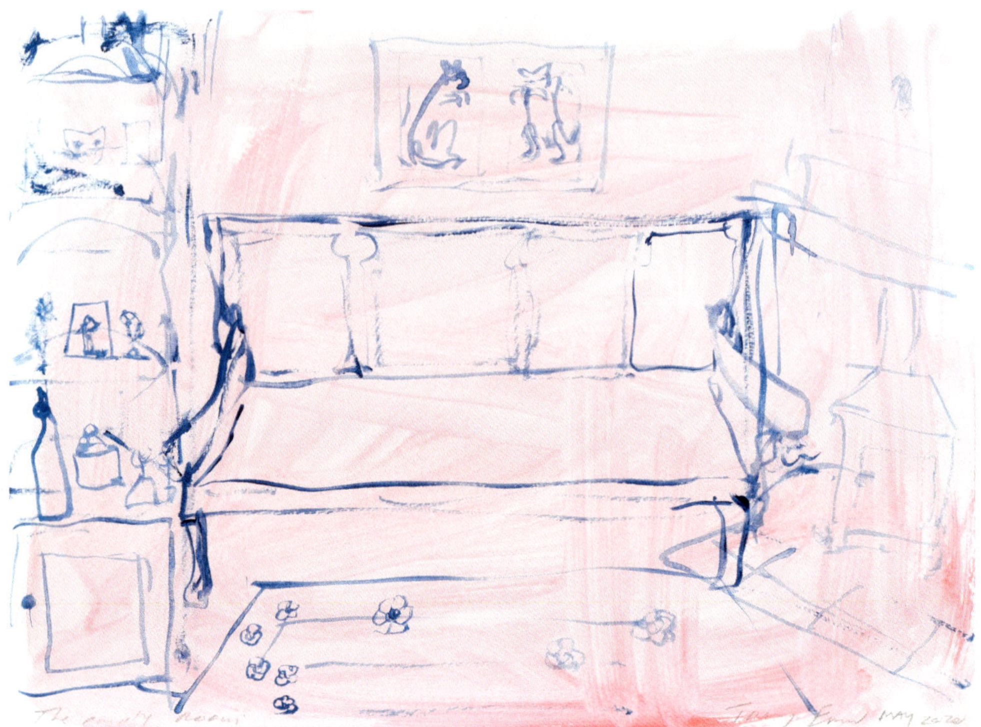

FIG. 6 *The Empty Room*, 2020. Gouache on paper, 9⅜ x 12½ in. (23.9 x 31.9 cm). Private collection

is a figure who is comfortable with her position in space but who is nonetheless unsettled, caught in a condition of flux and irresolution. This is, to return to Nancy's words, a body "that moves away from itself" in simultaneous formation and dissolution, as the arc of the woman's knee repeats across the surface like a series of chronophotographic frames, and darker pools of ink indicate moments of rest where Emin's hand has paused before resuming its path. Indeed, the body "repeats its irrepeatable unicity" with repetition, becoming both the confirmation of presence and its undoing.[8] It is the same with Emin's work, not only within individual drawings with their overlays and recurring traces, but also in her invocation of the same subjects over the years. *Filling up The empty Room* is joined, for example, by *The Empty Room* (fig. 6) also from 2020, an identical composition except here there is no occupant. Which comes first, absence or arrival? Must the act of being present be taken up again and again?

This same "coming and going of presence" characterizes the monotypes, in which the hesitant figures, however isolated, remain inextricably connected to the world outside them. By their nature, monotypes are spontaneous, leaving no chance for adjustments, and Emin's hastily sketched figures often bear the trace of their own registration, smudges of ink manifest in the white space around them. *If I could just go back + start again* (fig. 7) reads the title of a 1995 monotype in which a woman stands in the center of the page, her thin arms clasped to her sides and head awkwardly tilted as she stares into the distance. Alone in space, she reaches into the void much like the entreating figure with outstretched arms in *And Then you left me*. The invisible force emanating from these figures is made palpable in another monotype from this period titled *My Mind 1978* (fig. 8). Here, a solitary figure stands naked save for a thin line that reaches horizontally from her forehead, culminating in a seismographic-type scrawl to her left (her thoughts, her spirit?). It may not be possible to start again (to borrow Emin's title), but there is also no such thing as resolution in this universe. Rather, there is only suspension, as bodies hover ghostlike, between here and there.

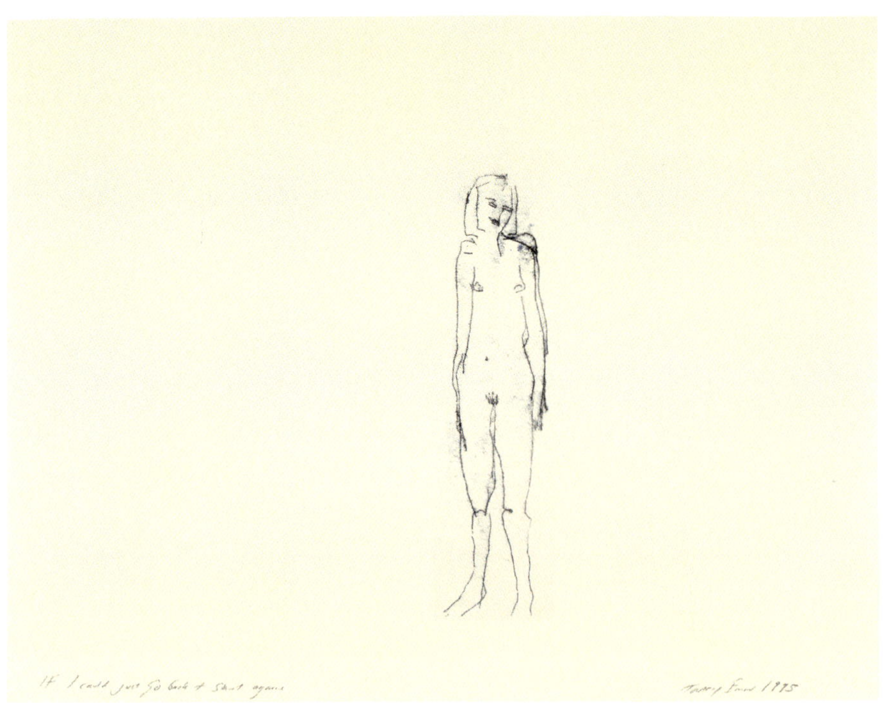

FIG. 7 *If I could just go back + start again*, 1995. Monoprint, 25⅝ x 32 in. (65 x 81.5 cm). Tracey Emin Archive

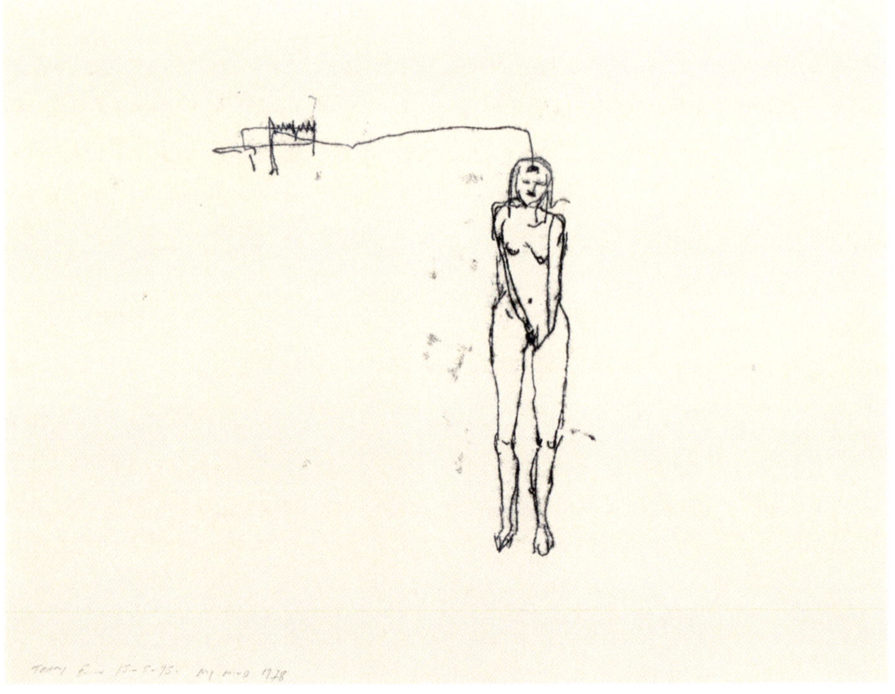

FIG. 8 *My Mind 1978*, 1995. Monoprint, 22⅞ x 29½ in. (58 x 75 cm). Private collection

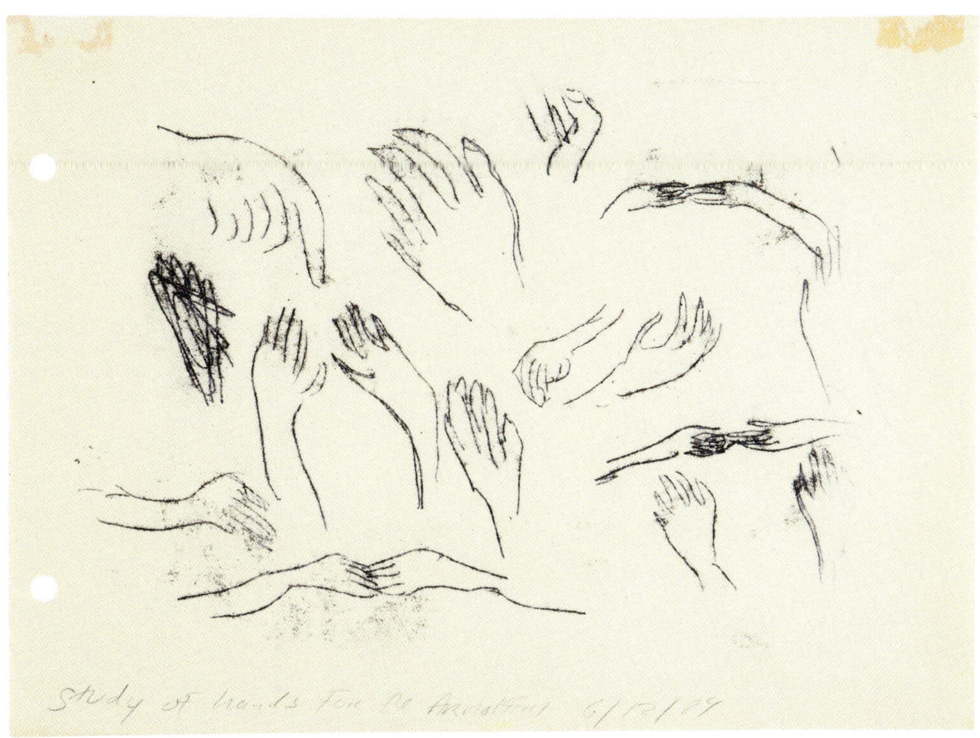

FIG. 9 *Study of Hands for The Arnolfini*, 1989. Monoprint, 12 x 16 in. (30.5 x 40.8 cm). Tracey Emin Archive

Emin has spoken frequently about her belief in the supernatural and her awareness since childhood of other "atmospheres, entities, feelings" that exist alongside the material universe.[9] Notably, her earliest monotypes, dating from the late 1980s, are filled with religious motifs — from invocations of the Deposition to Christ on the Cross to renderings of supplicating hands and feet. When I asked Emin about this body of work, she explained that it stemmed from the fact, during these years, that she used to regularly pass by the National Gallery on her way to the Royal Academy of Art and spent her days making drawings after icons and other religious paintings. But her attraction to this kind of imagery can't be dismissed as a mere product of circumstance. Indeed, in the 2009 book *One Thousand Drawings*, religious scenes continue to appear into the late 1990s, suggesting a relationship between religious subjects and her larger body of work. A page of repeating hands lifted up in prayerful application after the Arnolfini wedding portrait (fig. 9) presages a scene of a couple in bed protected by angels overhead, their arms outstretched (fig. 10), while this drawing

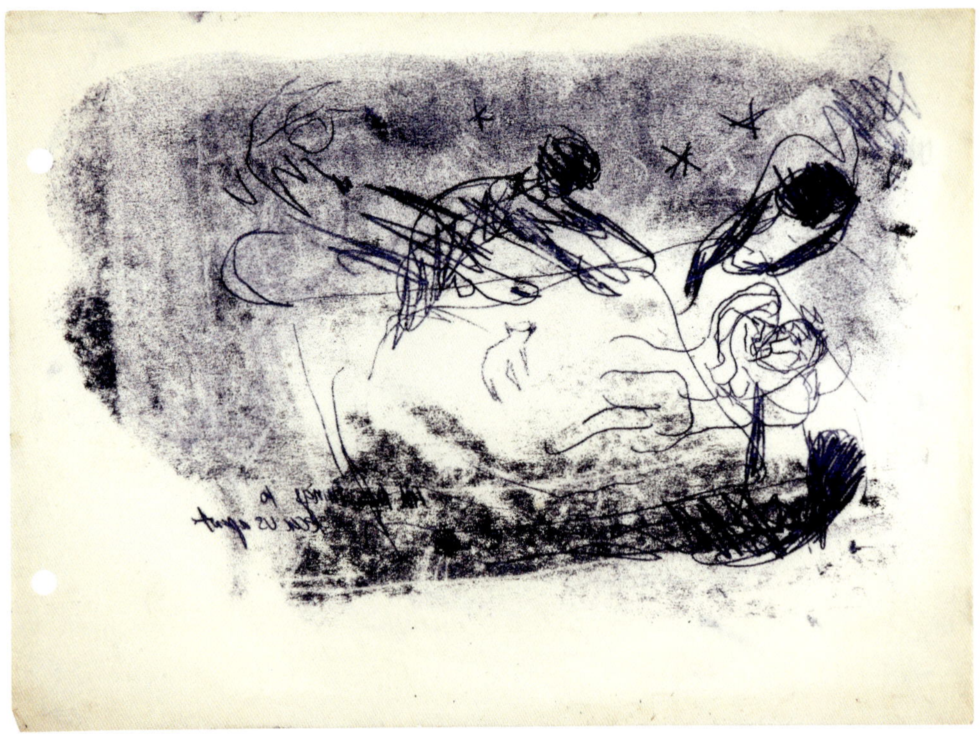

FIG. 10 *All things to tear us apart*, 1989. Monoprint, 12 x 16 in. (30.5 x 40.8 cm). Tracey Emin Archive

in turn echoes a scene of a couple embracing inside a floating balloon (fig. 11), whose simple diagonal thrust parallels a drawing of a dragonfly in flight (fig. 12). It is this same hesitant, bowing line that appears in her later monotypes featuring splayed limbs and arcing bodies, and that is perhaps most succinctly distilled in a drawing that appears midway through the book of a line extending from the bottom right to center top of the page before sloping down and culminating in a twisted knot. This purely abstract image perfectly encapsulates the ideas of aspiration, desire, and struggle that define Emin's work in general, in which art, sex, and spirituality all connect to a quest for a state of being beyond the confines of solitary, physical existence.

Emin's penchant for including text in her images reinforces this dynamic. On the one hand, her handwritten notations place her works in the confessional mode, with the inscriptions serving as a kind of personal commentary on the scenes depicted. And yet, to borrow from Jean-Luc Nancy, text in Emin's work is "something other than decipherment" and much more akin to a distinct release of "discharges, abandonments, retreats." "A body is what cannot be

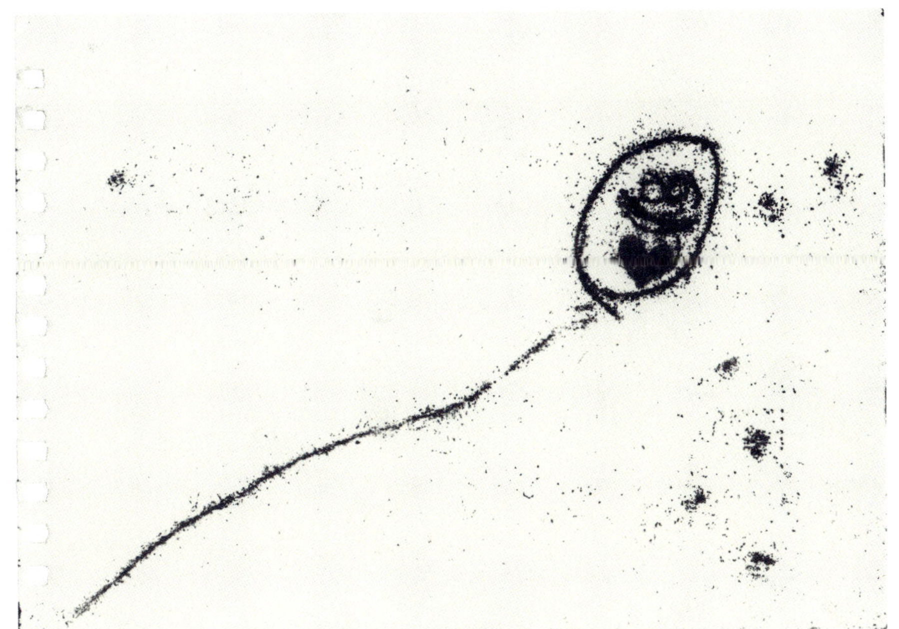

FIG. 11 *Yet to be titled (sperm with face)*, 1990. Monoprint, 7 x 5 in. (17.7 x 12.7 cm).
Tracey Emin Archive

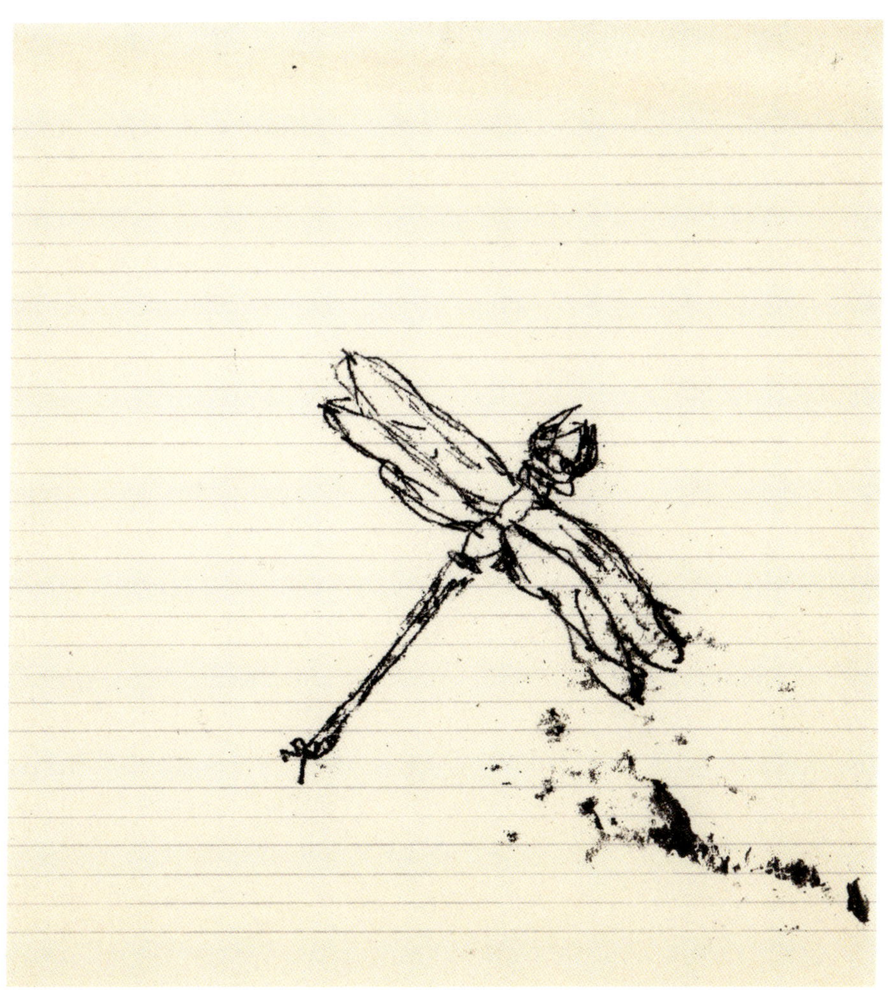

FIG. 12 *Untitled* from *Monoprint Diary*, 1991. Monoprint, 9¼ x 8¼ in. (23.5 x 21 cm).
Private collection

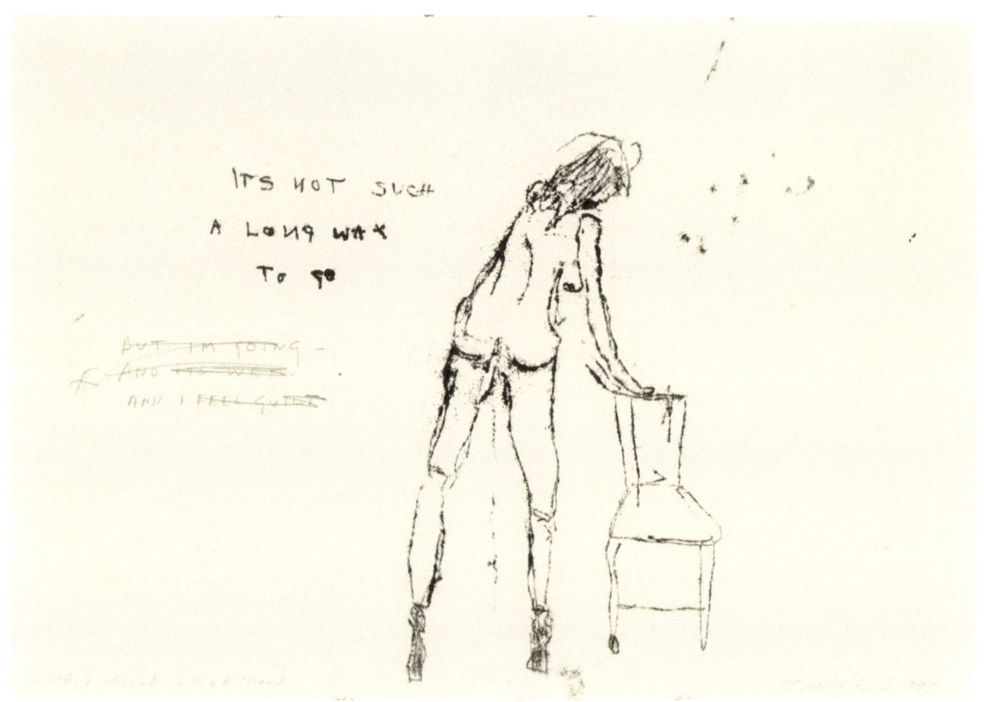

FIG. 13 *Walking Drunk in High Shoes*, 1998. Monoprint, 22⅞ x 31⅛ (58 x 81 cm). Private collection

read in a writing," observes Nancy, what remains "simply there . . . simply posited, weighed, weighty."[10] In much the same way, text and body reside on Emin's surfaces as two distinct modes that respond to yet inevitably miss each other. Much has been said about the spelling errors, backward letters, and crossings out that infiltrate Emin's script, particularly in the early monotypes.[11] Statements are made only to be invalidated, as in the 1998 monotype *Walking Drunk in High Shoes* (fig. 13), in which the penned phrase "ITS NOT SUCH A LONG WAY TO GO" is undone by the image of a teetering woman clinging to a chair for support and the additional halting lines — "I feel quite," "But I'm going," "And" — in crossed-out pencil additions.

Midway through *One Thousand Drawings* there appears an otherwise blank ruled sheet with the words "THE END," the *N* written backward (fig. 14). It is the final page of a notebook from 1990, which Emin has inserted in the book, but in this context the declarative culminating statement loses its authority as the drawings resume their inexorable flow. At the same time, the backward *N* resists the word's leftward-leaning slant and the book's progression. There is no going back and starting again but there is also no conclusion in Emin's universe. And this is as it should be. Emin's is a constant quest, however painful, an ongoing "birth to presence" accompanied by all the joys and sorrows that life, and what lies beyond it, contain.

FIG. 14 *Untitled* from *Monoprint Diary*, 1991. Monoprint, 9¼ x 8¼ in. (23.5 x 21 cm). Private collection

NOTES

1. Tracey Emin, in conversation with the author (June 26, 2024).
2. Jean-Luc Nancy, *The Birth to Presence*, trans. Brian Holmes and others (Redwood City, CA: Stanford University Press, 1993), 2.
3. Nancy, *Birth to Presence*, 353.
4. Tracey Emin, *Tracey Emin: Strangeland* (London: Hodder & Stoughton, 2005), 37; 36; 132.
5. Tracey Emin, interview by Charles M. Schultz, *The Brooklyn Rail* (December 23 – January 24, 2024), https://brooklynrail.org/2023/12/art/Tracey-Emin-with-Charles-M-Schultz.
6. Tracey Emin, "Ghosts of My Past," *The Guardian* (May 24, 2009), https://www.theguardian.com/artanddesign/2009/may/25/tracey-emin-drawing-art.
7. Emin, in conversation with the author.
8. Nancy, 353.
9. Tracey Emin, interview with Simon Joseph Jones, "A Good Art Is Hard to Find," *High Profiles* (2024), https://highprofiles.info/interview/tracey-emin/.
10. Nancy, 198–200.
11. For two excellent essays on Emin and language, see Chris Townsend, "Heart of Glass: Reflection, Reprise and Riposte in Self-Representation," in *The Art of Tracey Emin*, ed. Mandy Merck and Chris Townsend (London: Thames & Hudson, 2002), 79–101, and Camilla Jalving, "'It was just me, Tracey': Strategies of Self-Presentation in the Art of Tracey Emin," in *Art into Life: Essays on Tracey Emin*, ed. Alexandra Kokoli and Deborah Cherry (London: Bloomsbury Visual Arts, 2020), 29–40.

DRAWINGS

Plates 23–35

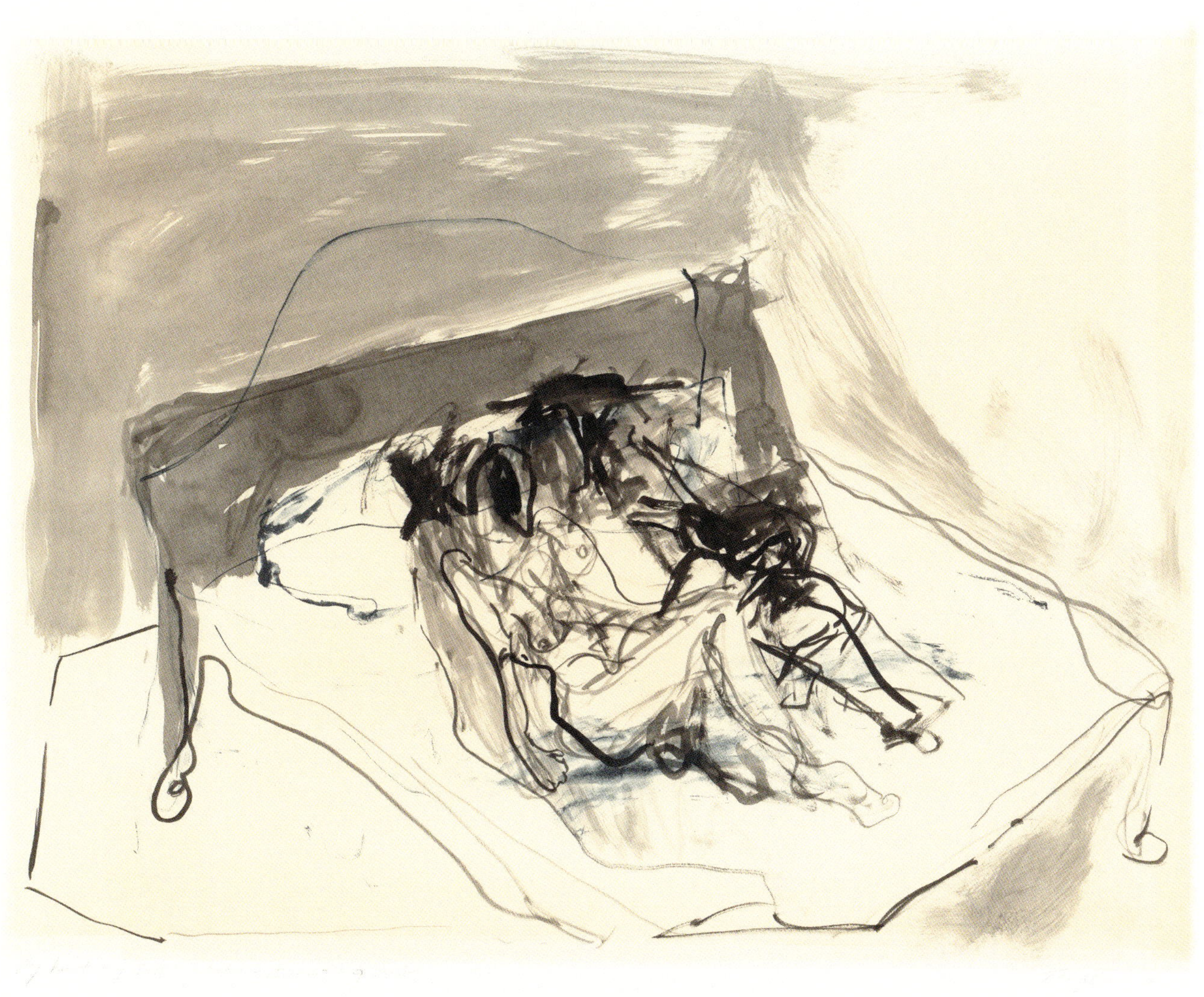

PLATE 23

***My heart my soul my body — Every — Thing shook* 2021**

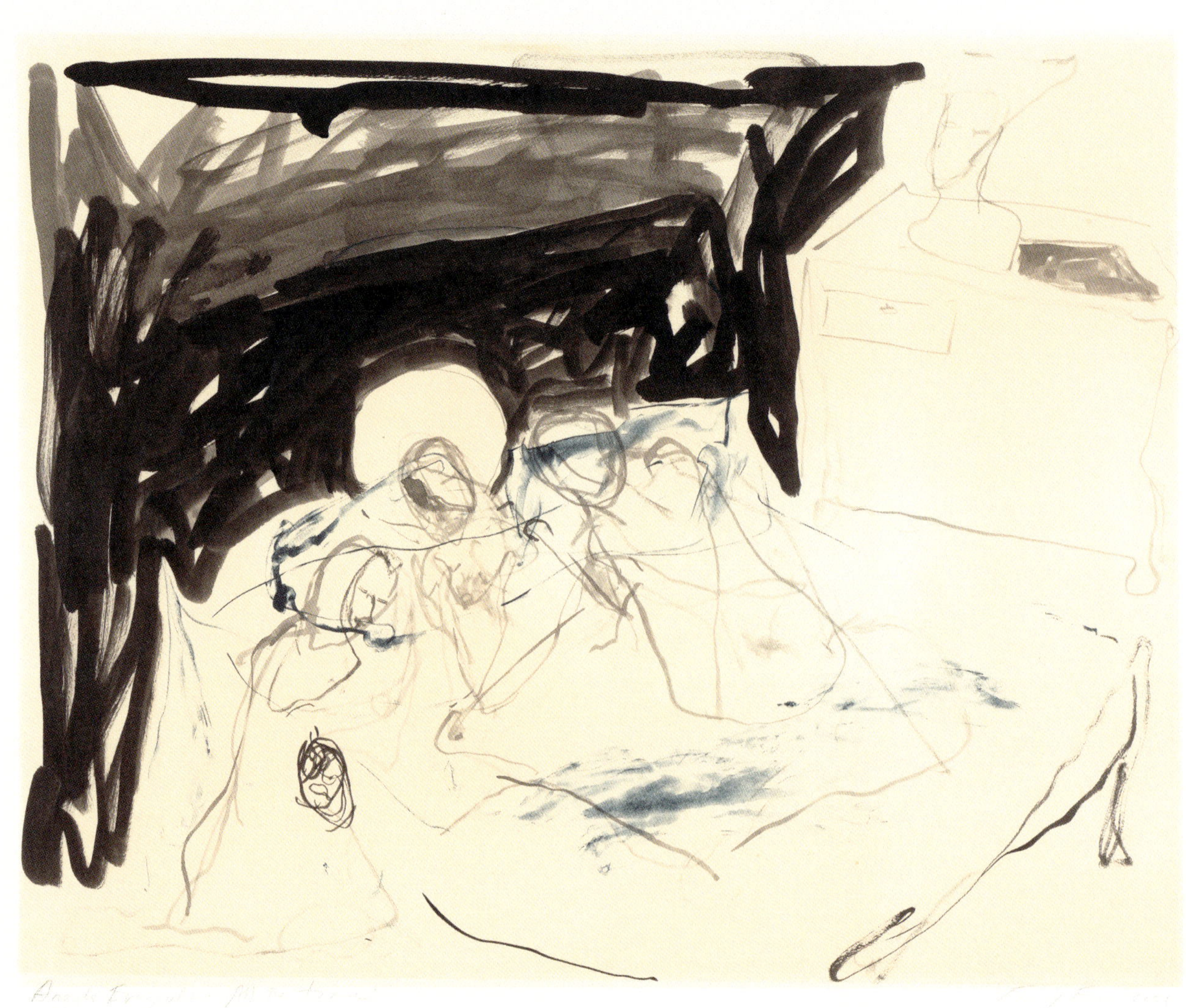

PLATE 24

Angels Every where All the time 2021

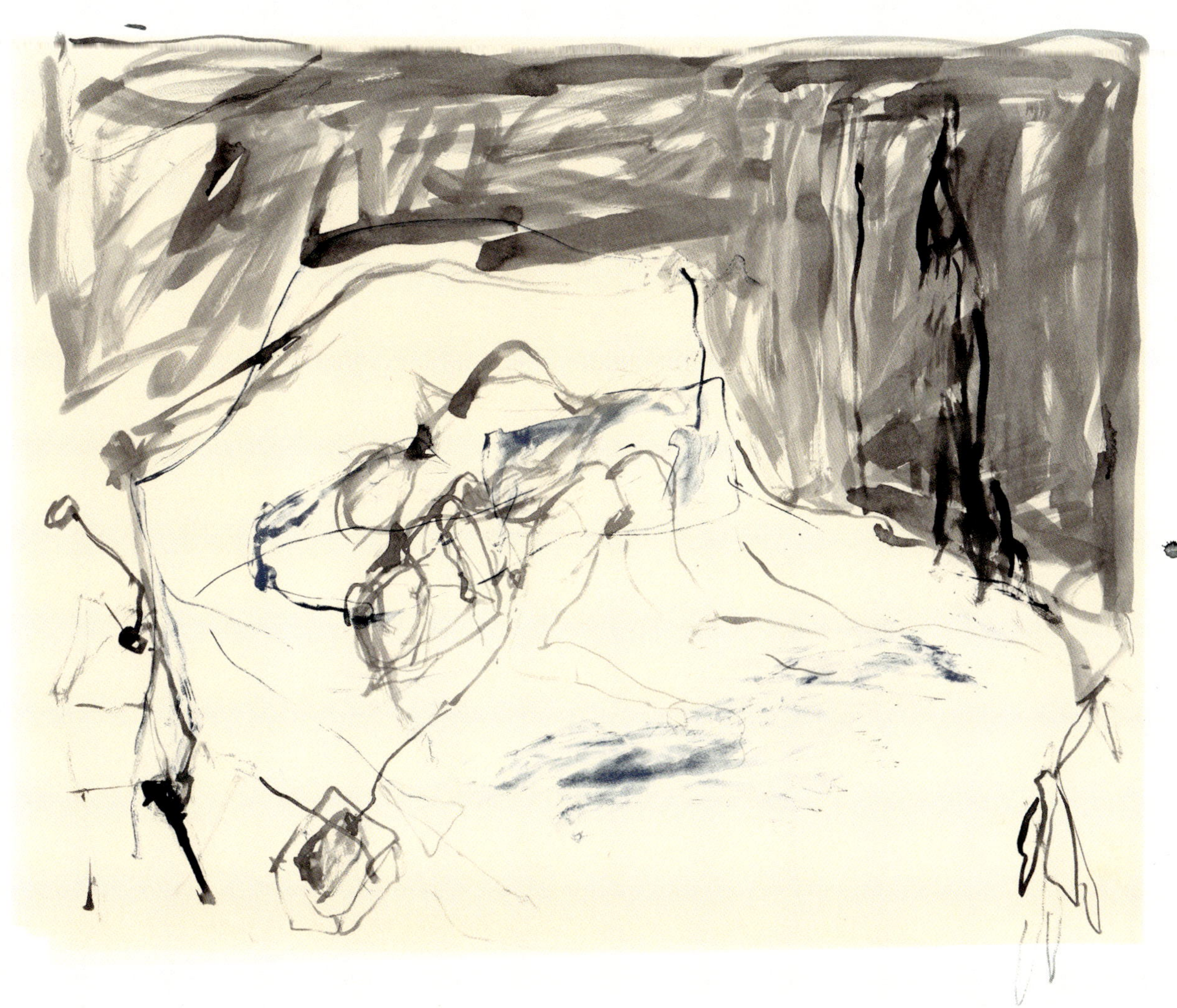

PLATE 25

Some Things make No difference 2022

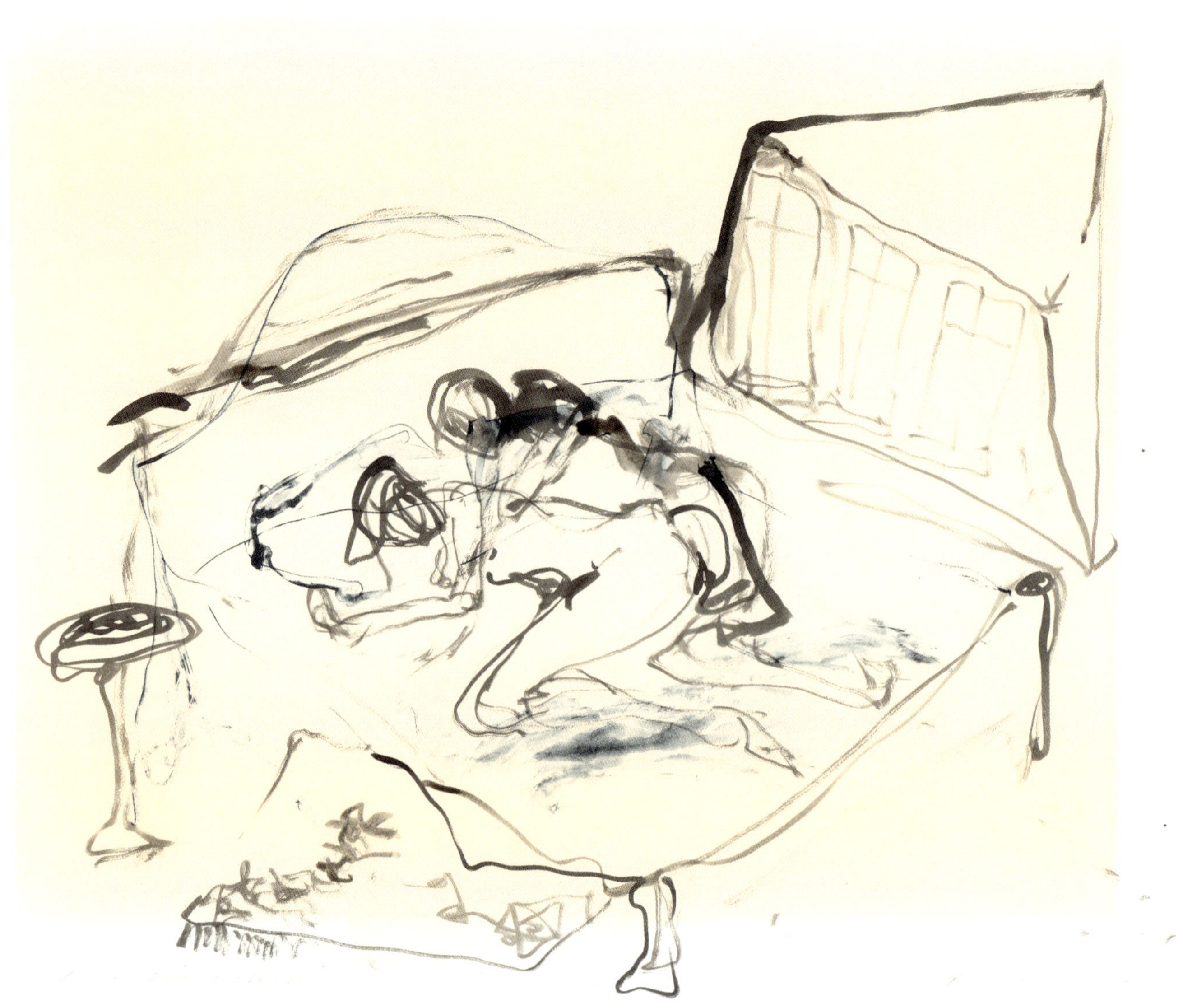

You were supposed to have loved me 2023

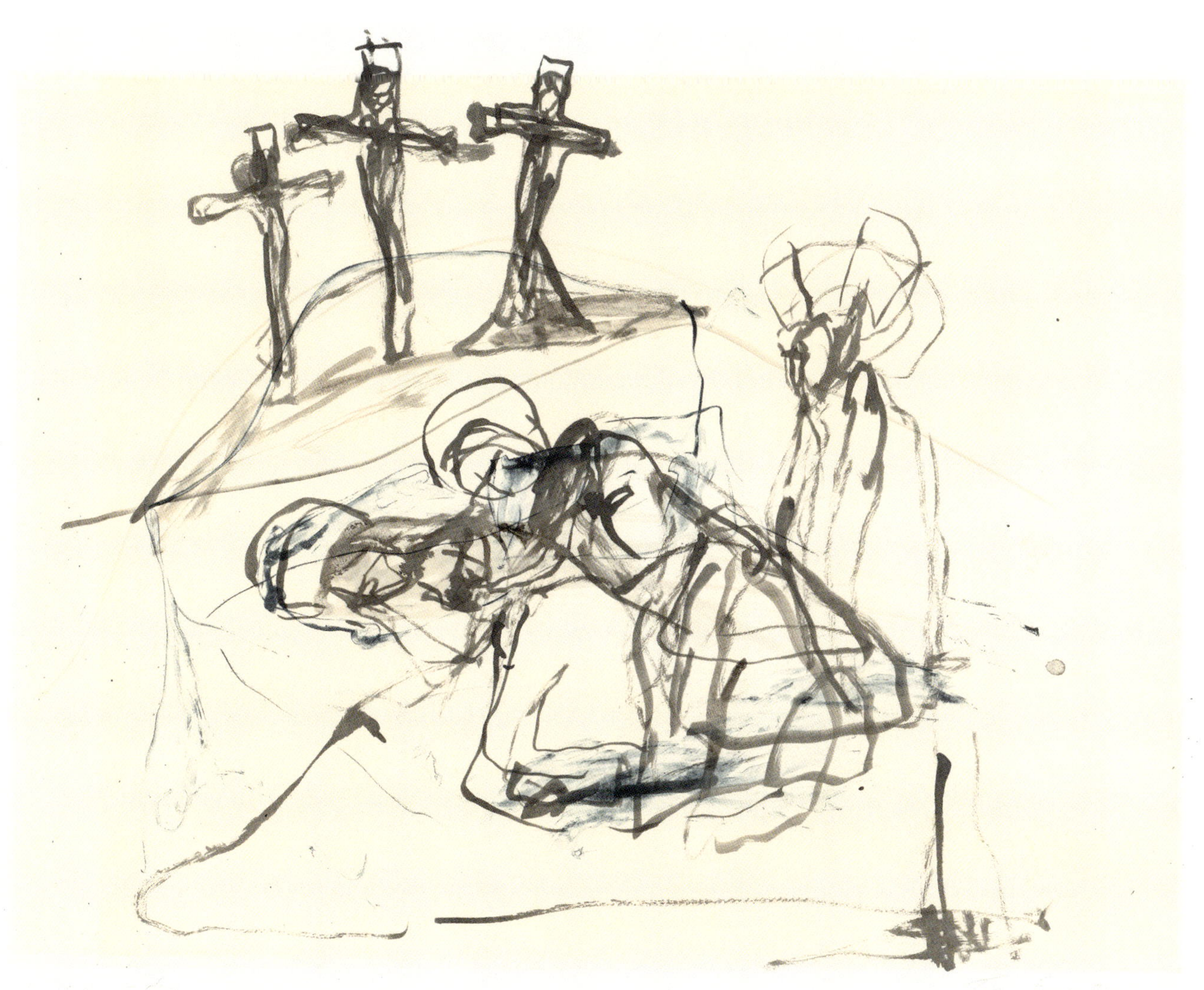

PLATE 27

In The darkest days 2023

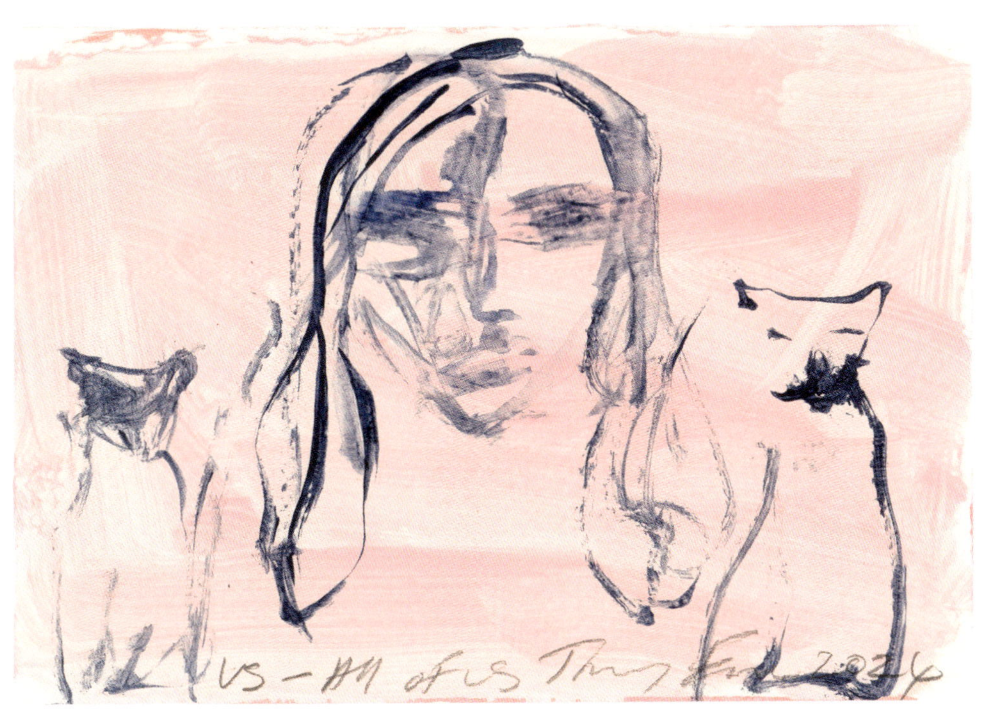

PLATE 28

US — All of Us 2024

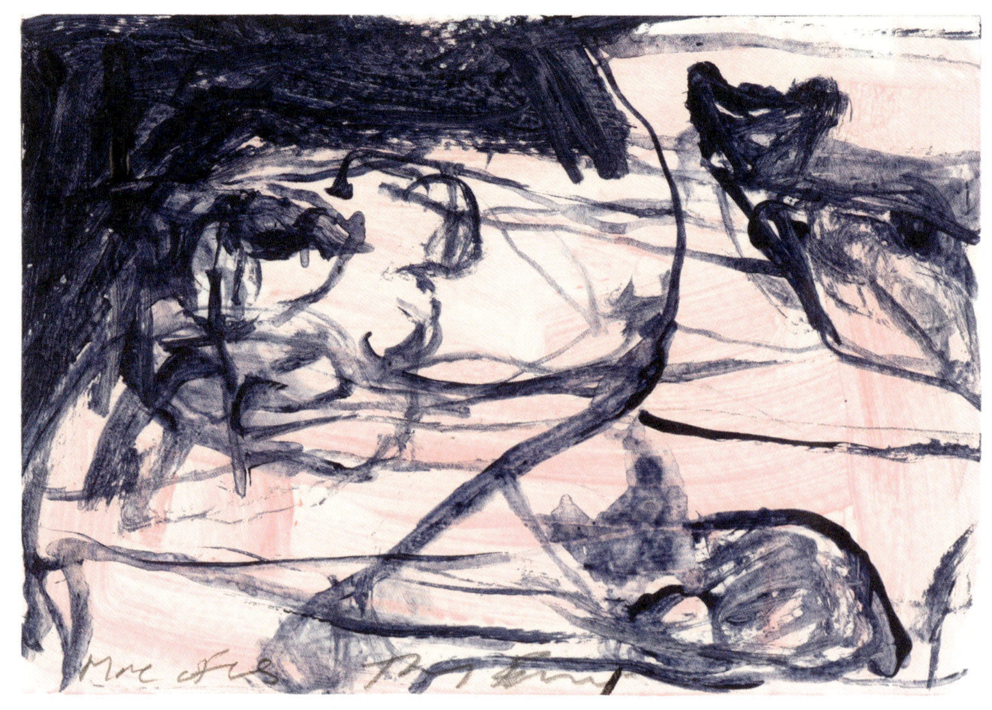

PLATE 29

More Of Us 2024

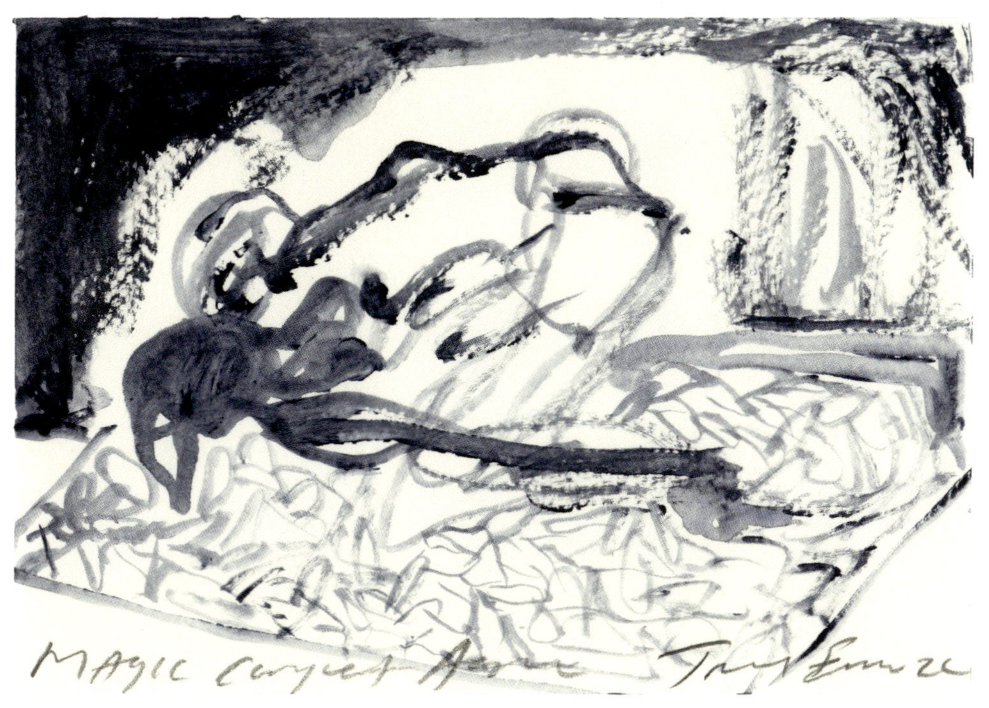

PLATE 30

***MAGIC Carpet Again* 2024**

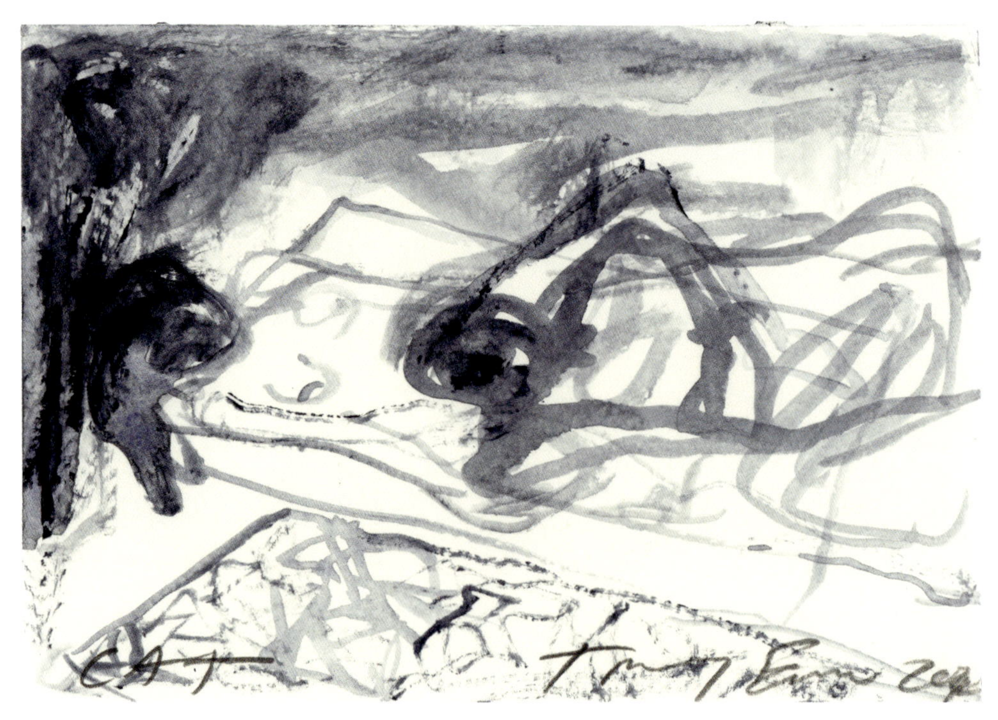

PLATE 31

CAT **2024**

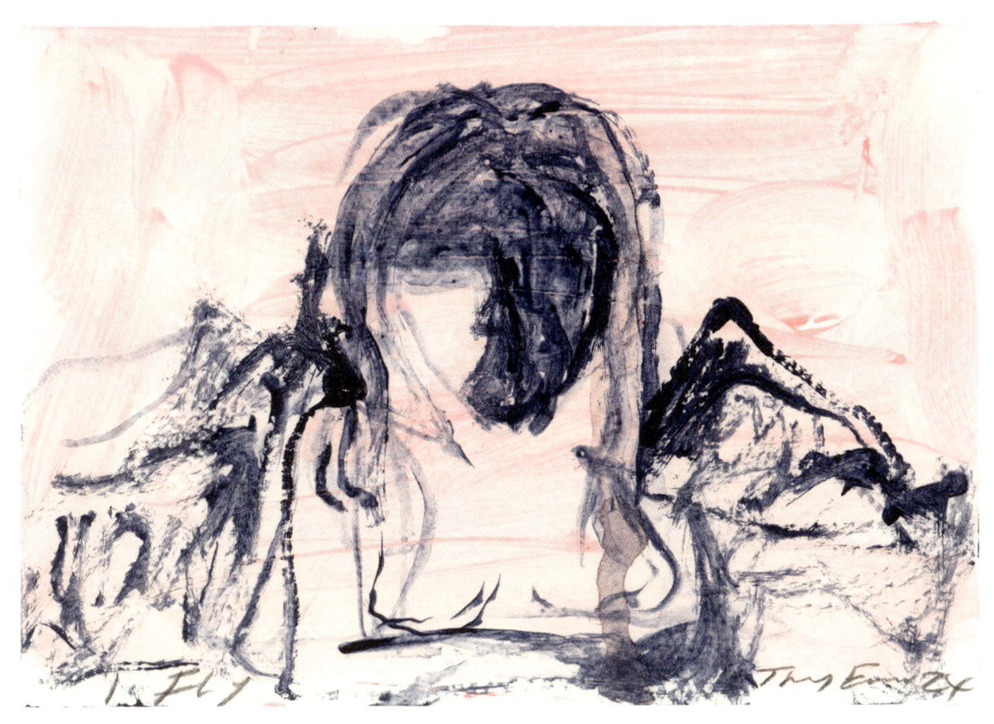

PLATE 32

I Fly 2024

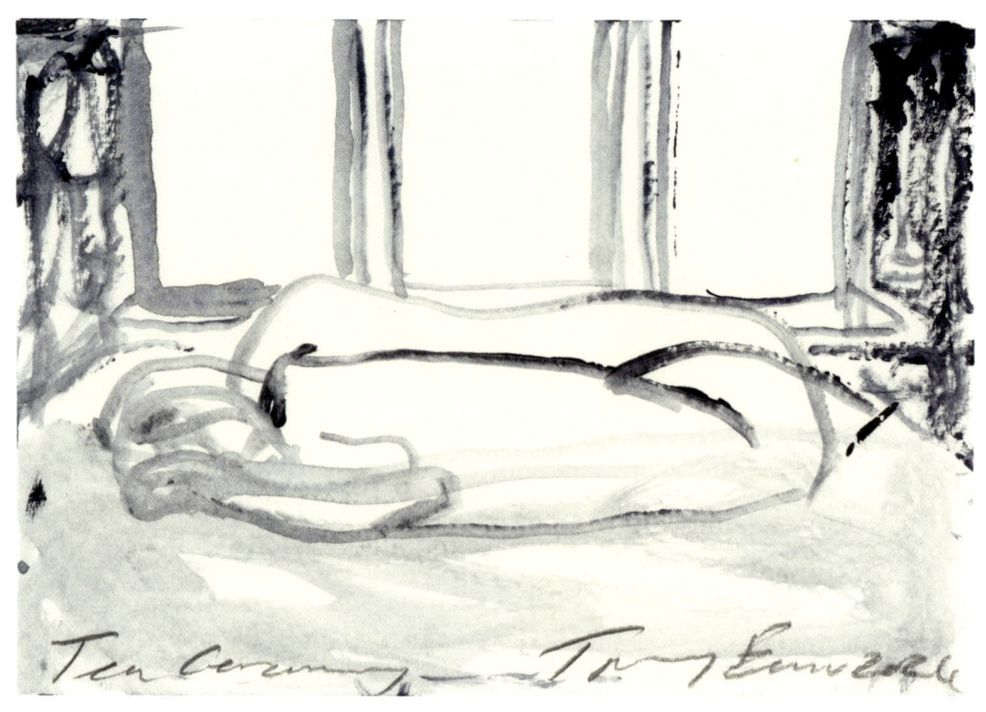

PLATE 33

Tea Ceremony 2024

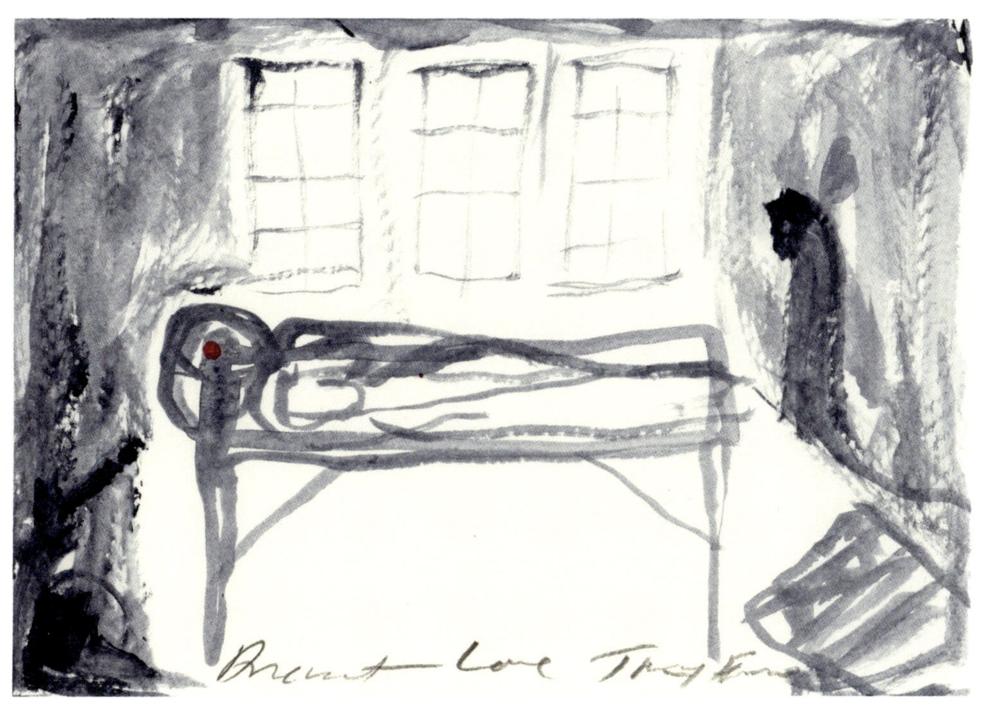

PLATE 34

***Ancient Love* 2024**

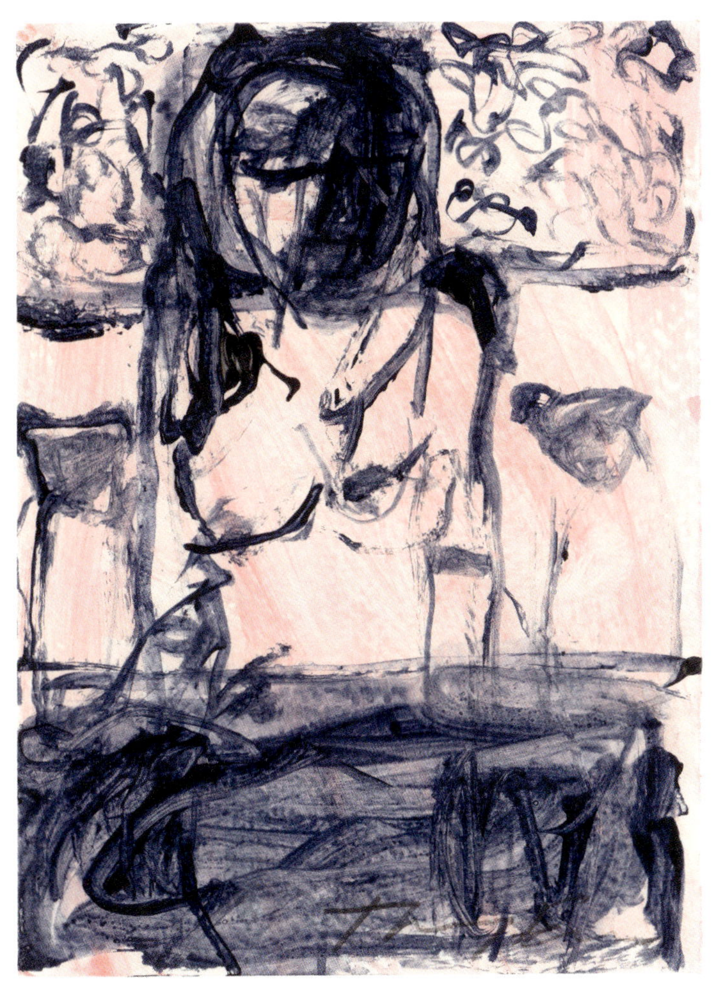

PLATE 35

I Saw you looking at me 2024

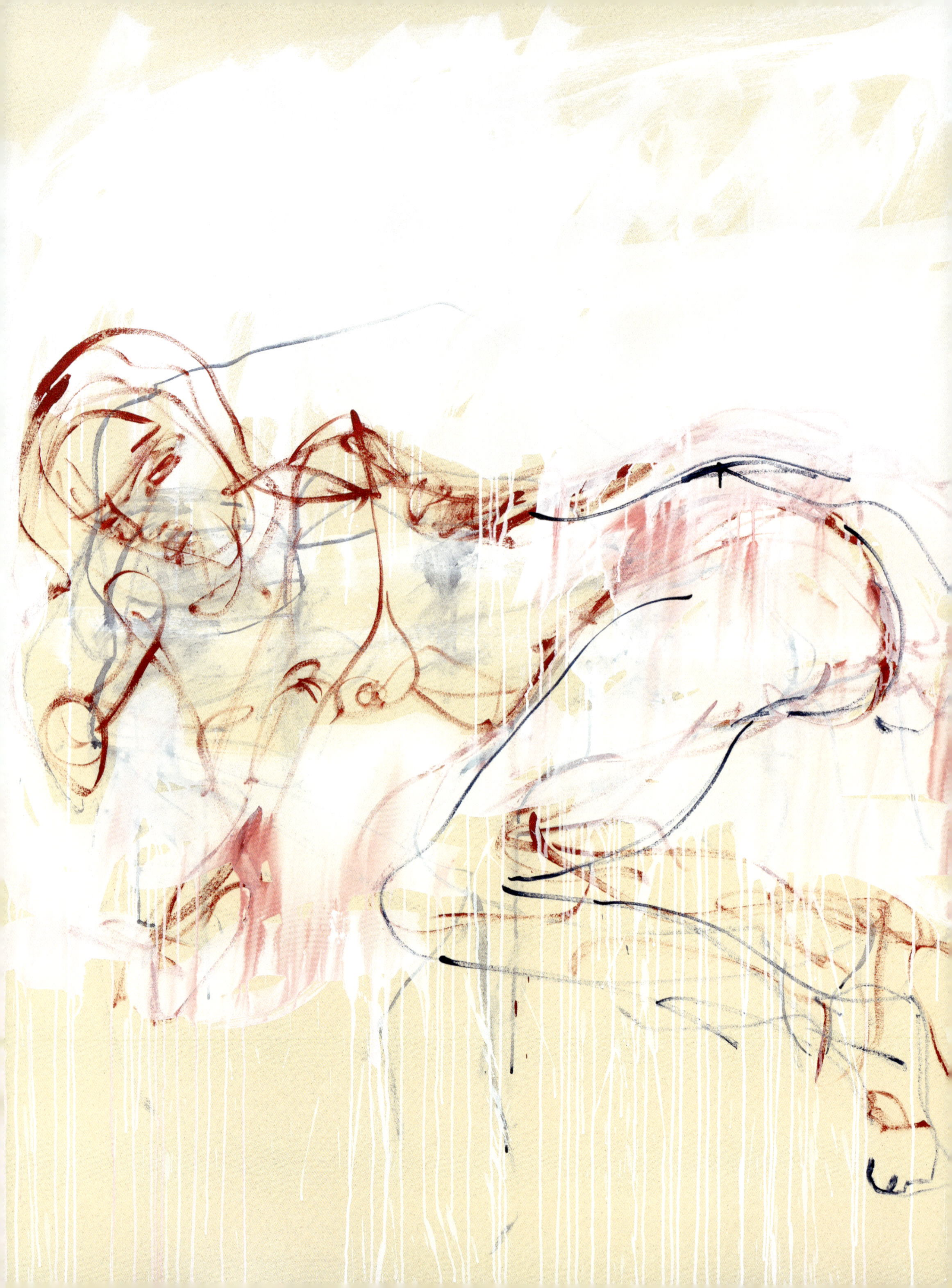

PAINTING IS REAL:
TRACEY EMIN IN CONVERSATION

Courtney J. Martin

In the last sentences of her 2005 memoir, Strangeland, *Tracey Emin recounts a visit to the National Museum in Oslo to view Edvard Munch's* The Scream *(1893):*

> My eyes hurt; they were swollen puffy balls. I hadn't eaten or slept properly in weeks and there I was, in Norway, paying homage to my favorite painting. But paying homage wasn't enough, I wanted to jump inside the picture and cradle *The Scream* in my arms. Another lost soul.

Emin's recollection of the experience of seeing The Scream *speaks to the way in which painting—her own and that of others—has captivated her and motivated her practice for more than thirty-five years. Since she entered the Royal College of Art in 1987, key turning points in her career—a retreat from painting in the 1990s, the 2007 Venice Biennale, a remarkable exhibition of her own and Munch's work in 2020–22—and life have marked her engagement with and disengagement from the medium. For Emin the ability to paint was as hard won as the results have been sometimes easy to destroy. In June 2024 we met in her home and studio in London to discuss her evolution not simply as an artist but as a painter. On the following evening, the Royal Academy of Arts would honor her painting* Did it Ever Get Any Better *with the Charles Wollaston Award for "most distinguished work" in its 255th Summer Exhibition. This award, alongside recent well-received exhibitions of her paintings and the opening of her eponymous foundation for artists in her hometown of Margate, suggest that she can both control and excel in this medium for herself and for others.*

Did it Ever Get Any Better, 2024. Acrylic on canvas, 71¾ x 59⅞ in. (182.3 x 152.2 cm). Tracey Emin Archive

 When did you start painting?

TE That's a complicated subject. I did a printmaking degree at Maidstone College of Art starting in 1983 and a painting Master's at the Royal College of Art starting in 1987. I wanted to do painting because I couldn't paint. I could make pictures with paint — I made tiny paintings on board and these big paintings with screen ink in 1983 or '84 or whatever. But I never had any money to buy oil paint. I never had proper brushes. I didn't know how to mix oil paint. I didn't know how to use linseed oil. I didn't know how to stretch or prime a canvas. I wanted to learn those things, so I went to the Royal College of Art to learn how to paint. And I did — it was brilliant. I learned many things, and it set me up for painting. But then just after I left the Royal College of Art, in 1990, I got pregnant, and I couldn't stand the smell of oil paint or linseed oil, and I had to stop painting. And then I felt too guilty to paint anymore. I just couldn't do it.

CJM Why did you feel guilty?

TE About the abortion. I didn't feel guilty, like, I'm a bad person. I felt bereft. And I thought that if I'd been a good artist or a good painter then maybe I wouldn't have had the abortion. But I had the abortion because there was no way I could look after a child on my own. Also, with my background, I wasn't going to go all the way through the Royal College of Art, get this amazing education, learn to paint, and then be a single mother. I wasn't going to do that. It was impossible. I understood that I was completely alone as a human being and as a creator. Also, in the '90s it was really hard to be a painter, especially a figurative painter. Everything was sort of stacked against me, so I stopped painting but I carried on drawing. It wasn't like I wanted a career in painting. I wanted to be an artist.

CJM Why would you have been a figurative painter?

TE Because the painters who influenced me — from Edvard Munch to Egon Schiele to Käthe Kollwitz — were all figurative, expressionist artists. I suppose I was quite naïve and my art education was kind of weird. I had left school at thirteen, when I was very young. I wasn't an educated person going to art school. I got into art school without any qualifications, just doing what I loved, and loving what I loved. My art education at Maidstone was pretty radical and fantastic. At the Royal College of Art it was much more conservative, slightly fuddy-duddy, and quite macho, in a way.

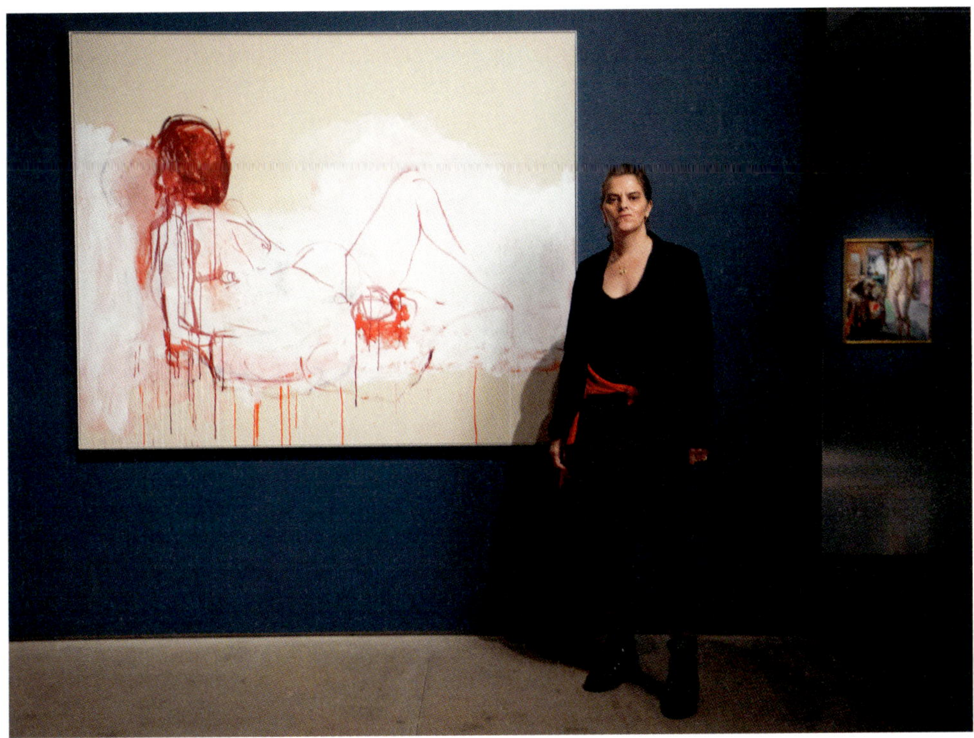

Tracey Emin with *This is life without you — You made me Feel like This* (2018), at *Tracey Emin / Edvard Munch: The Loneliness of the Soul*, Royal Academy of Arts, London, 2021

CJM For most artists entering graduate programs, there's an assumption that they already have the skill, and at the graduate level, they will do the theory, or learn complex concepts, or work out an idea. What you experienced in graduate school — learning how to paint — is unusual.

TE Well, there was painting in me. I was a really good printmaker, technically, and really good at drawing. In my interview at the Royal College of Art, when they saw my seven sketchbooks — in the old days you had to have seven sketchbooks, but no one had seven sketchbooks — apparently they went, "We've got one! We found one. We found someone with the sketchbooks!" Then they looked at my paintings, and they said they had never seen such bad paintings. I was using screen ink to paint — gooey, gunky screen ink. When I had my interview, I told them, "I can't paint. That's why I want to come here. I want to learn to paint." They said it was so honest and refreshing. I also told them I wanted to study with Ken Kiff [1935–2001] as a tutor. So they see this girl, who's kind of a bit wild and everything, with two really good reasons for wanting to go to the Royal College of Art

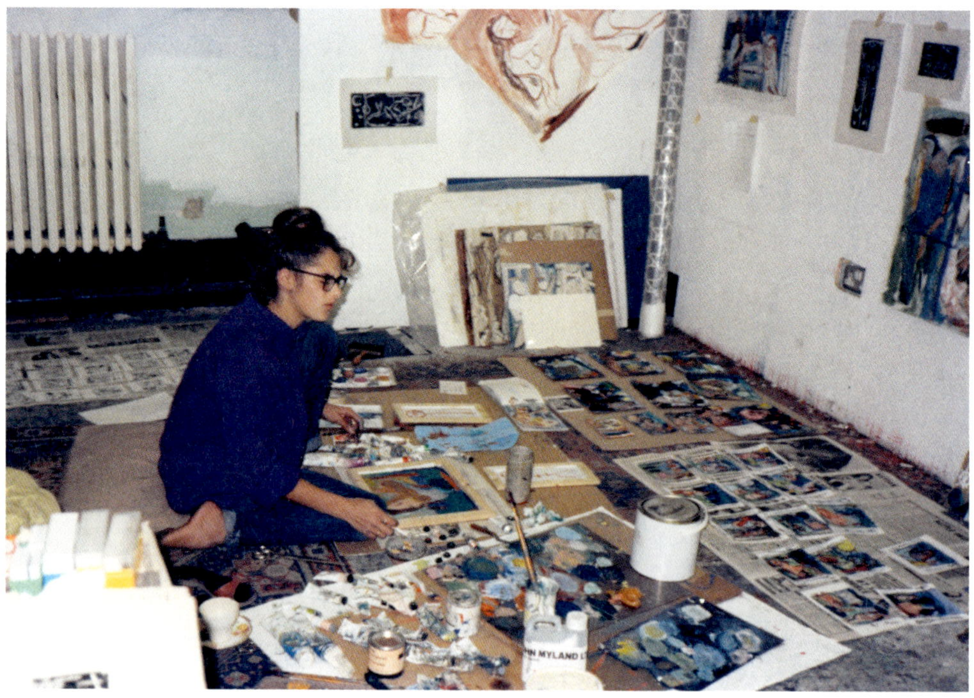

Tracey Emin in her studio, Royal College of Art, London, 1989

that have got nothing to do with career, with success, with wanting to be a well-known artist, with putting art in a gallery, with money. My reasons were pure.

Then, at the end of the first year, I still wasn't really painting. I was doing hundreds of watercolors, but you had to do an oil painting to be in the painting school at Royal College of Art. So I went after this amazing summer travel grant, but they said, "You're not going anywhere. You have to stay here. You can have as much canvas, as much wood, for as many stretchers as you want. The technician will help you twice a day, just you. And you'll have tutors you choose come in twice a week."

So that summer I studied with Ken and Alan Miller [1941–2009]. Alan Miller taught me how to cut and miter and make my own stretchers and how to make beautiful gesso grounds. With Ken, I learned about mixing colors, how to use linseed oil, and egg tempera. So I had really good instruction and by the end of the summer I'd done my first really big oil painting and I was off and running. It was brilliant. I spent the next year just doing oil paintings. I was still really influenced by Munch but also by the Turkish side of my family, by my own ancestry. My paintings were like a cross between Munch and Byzantine frescos, really kind of strange.

CJM Were you also going to galleries at this point? I think you were living in London.

TE Yeah, I lived at Elephant and Castle. I'd get the 53 bus every morning to Westminster and get in the tube to South Kensington. But about twice a week I'd get the bus to Trafalgar Square, go to the National Gallery, and spend time with the early and mid-Renaissance paintings and altarpieces. They were in the basement then—all this beautiful gold in the basement. So I'd go and I'd sketch them, and when I left, I would imagine my paintings in the next room. And I'd go, "Ooh." I'd shudder.

CJM Shudder out of fear?

TE Shudder and think, Oh, I'm never going to make it. My competitor was early Renaissance paintings. It wasn't Gerhard Richter, or whatever the big thing was then. My target was something you can't actually compete with. I'd use subjects like the Wedding at Cana or the Last Supper, or the Head of John the Baptist, and reinvent them. These were religious drawings. I'd also gotten into classical music for the first time in my life — going from rock 'n' roll to Bach. I'd made this massive mental leap for myself, into a place that I never knew was possible for me. So, at the Royal College of Art, I got a sense of classic, classic, classics. It was amazing, but to be quite honest, the Royal College of Art probably wasn't the right place for that. There was a lot of big, abstract painting going on, and I was just not cutting it. It was a rather difficult time for me. I don't want to use these words, because it's derogatory, but I was kind of a working-class mascot. I kind of crept in through the back door. They thought, Well, we've got one. That's our quota. We ticked our box. Also, my second subject was sacred geometry and forgotten knowledge, with Keith Critchlow [1933–2020].

CJM Yes, that would set you apart, too. Keith Critchlow is an interesting figure in your education because by the time that you're meeting him, he doesn't represent what's being taught.

TE No, but Keith Critchlow was teaching me the right stuff. People who studied with Keith ended up doing stained glass, Islamic patterns, things like that. It was weird to be the person from painting sitting in those lectures, but I loved sacred geometry and Sufi mysticism and 13th-century esoteric philosophy. It was perfect for me, but it didn't really coincide.

Then when I left the Royal College of Art, I did a part-time philosophy course, which was brilliant. Because I left school early, my brain had a massive wedge that was ready to be filled. And philosophy did that. When you do a philosophy course you have to learn things you don't like. You have to take them on board, mentally, and deal with them. You can't say, I don't like this. I'm not going to process it. You have to process it, and learn it, say why you don't like it, to be able to move on to the next level of thought.

Suddenly, I went from not being able to understand anything conceptual or minimal in art to, as if overnight, understanding anything I looked at. Things I thought I didn't like, like Agnes Martin or Robert Ryman, I was now thinking, Wow, that's pretty good. I feel this. I'd always liked Rothko, though, who I stumbled across by chance. It's one of my favorite stories. The first time I went to the Tate, I was twenty-two, and I was looking for their Munch painting [*The Sick Child*, 1907] and I came across this pink and yellow abstract painting by Rothko [*Untitled*, c. 1950–52], I was just struck. I just stood there and then I sat on a bench and just cried and cried. I'd never seen a Rothko before in my life. I didn't like abstract painting. I liked expressionism. I was looking for my Munch painting, a sick girl.

CJM Did you understand the spiritual side of Rothko in that moment?

TE I understood something. When I went back to college, I went to the library, looked up Rothko, and couldn't believe what I saw and what I read. I was looking at this book, which started off with his early, figurative paintings. They are so good, so beautiful, so magical. Then I read that he committed suicide, and I thought, Fucking hell. We know this now, but I understood it already, just looking at his painting at the Tate. I felt the sadness in the painting. That's why I was crying. I was feeling so pleased, or not pleased, but it was like I'd found a friend. That painting resonated with me. It hit me there, being for the first time at the Tate, in these rooms with art of this level, with this painting—I understood the journey I wanted to go on.

CJM I became aware of you as a painter with *Exorcism of the Last Painting I Ever Made,* which originated in Stockholm in 1996 at Galleri Andreas Brändström, came to the South London Art Gallery a year later, and was reinstalled at Faurschou in New York in 2023. For the initial work, you lived and painted in a room constructed within the gallery, visible to viewers through fish-eye lenses,

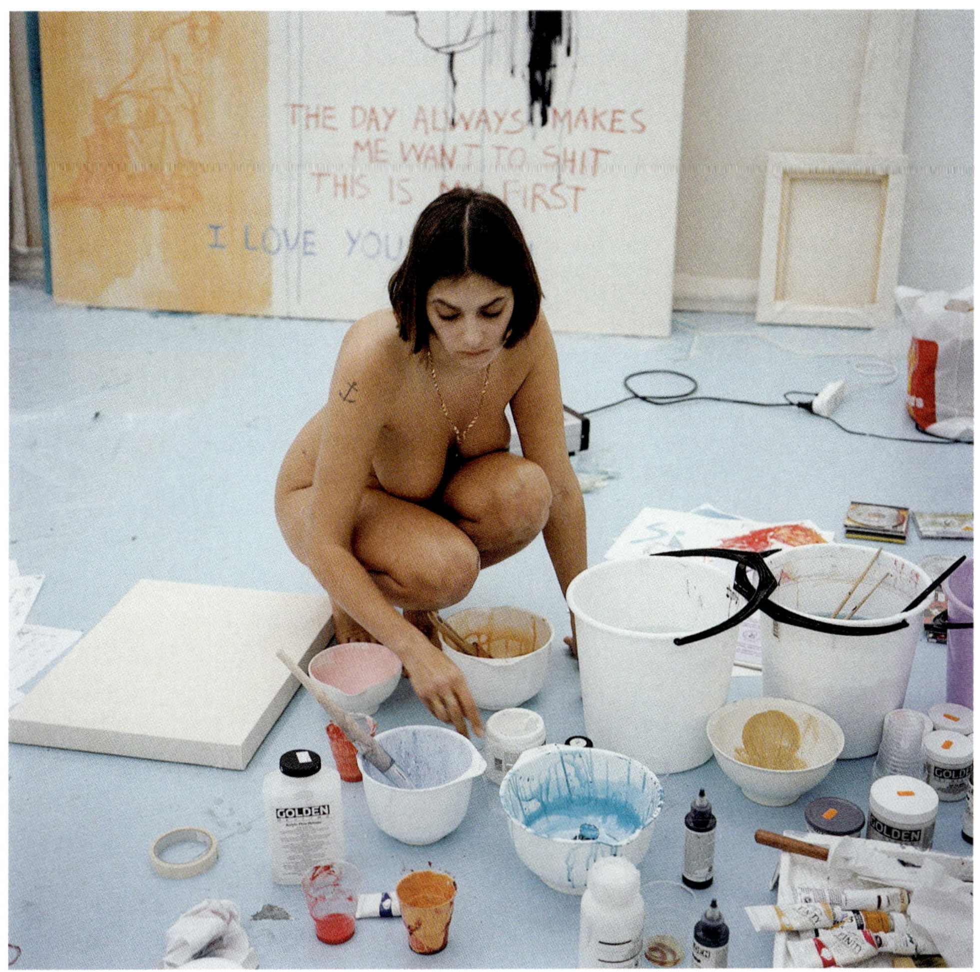

Naked Photos – Life Model Goes Mad I, 1996. Giclée print, 24¼ x 24 in. (61.5 x 61 cm)

for three weeks. You were thirty-three then. It was ten years after that moment in the Tate, but we can see now through the Faurschou show that there was so much you were about to inhabit. It's like you're about to jump off into something, but you don't know what at that moment.

TE When that project began, I hadn't painted since I was pregnant, six years earlier. My grandmother had died, and I was very upset. I hated my body. I was afraid to sleep. I was afraid of the dark. So I thought, I'm going to just sort all this out, in this three-week period. I painted naked so I could be with my body while people were looking at me. It was quite scary, the whole thing. For the first two days, I just sat there with *The Guardian* newspaper. I felt so fat. I felt so ugly. I thought my tits were like bongos hanging down. I just felt really weird. Now, when I look at those images, I think, Fucking hell! I had no idea I looked like that.

The photographs of me from that project are called *The Life Model Goes Mad*. I was really aware that I was my own model in everything that I did, my own muse. I painted my own history of art in that room. I did a Picasso, an Egon Schiele, and so on. Even though they all look like Tracey paintings now, I was channeling other artists. The Yves Klein paintings, for example, I loved those. That was a turning point for me. I don't care what anyone else says. I love them. They're sensual, sexual, fantastic, unapologetic. The most shocking thing about the Yves Klein paintings, the blue ones, is not what he's doing with the women, it's all the people standing around the edge with their bow ties and their cocktails.

CJM That they're just going on with everything while he uses women as "human paintbrushes."

TE Yes. Anyway, when I painted myself blue, when I did the first brushstroke on my leg, I heard someone yell, "She's doing that Yves Klein!" I couldn't see who was there, watching me, but I could hear everyone running to watch. It was phenomenal, but I wasn't doing it to be provocative. It was just part of my own history of art. It was quite empowering, looking at the whole of your own art history, and then being in a room, making it. I thought I would carry on painting after that, but I didn't.

CJM I've been wanting to ask you about that now for twenty years. Why did you stop painting again?

TE I did that project, and I had planned to burn all the work afterward, but the gallerist wouldn't let me. So it traveled around, like a sort of touring menagerie of a misfit, like a circus type of thing. It was totally out of context, totally weird. Also, I'd painted that work in acrylic for the first time ever because I didn't want to be in the room with all the oil paint, especially after having been pregnant and sick and vomiting. The project was about releasing myself not just with painting but as an artist. I wanted to understand that I made the right choice in having the abortion, that I'd done the right things, to not feel bad about myself in any way. The show is called *Exorcism of the Last Painting I Ever Made*. I had to exorcise these negative feelings and come full circle, come back into myself as an artist.

And, oh my God, did I come back with a vengeance. That was 1996. And I made *My Bed* in 1997. So, there you go. Bang. Big, giant, seminal piece of work. How many seminal pieces of art are made in history? Not many. How many have been made by women? Not many. How many are really ephemeral. Not many. And I had to defend and defend that bed. Everybody thought I was doing things to shock, to be provocative. But the bed, to me, was always like a painting. I used to say to people, "If it were a painting, you wouldn't make a fuss about it. Look at all the paintings in history, look at all the unruffled sheets, look at all the lovers' beds."

CJM What is painterly about the bed? Why is it a painting and not a sculpture?

TE Well, it is a sculpture. But when you paint, when you engage with the canvas, you've slipped into this chasm, this sort of vortex of space and time. It becomes something else. You are totally absorbed in it, and it's wrapping itself around you. You're a part of it. That's exactly how the bed is. The bed wrapped itself around me. It had smelled me, it had been me. My sweat was in it, my shit was on it, my blood was in it. My soul was seeped into that bed. A really good painting has even more of that absorption. It's only paint and canvas, it's just a brush. But it isn't. Over time I started to understand what painting was bringing out of me — the journey, the battle, the emotions. Subconsciously, I stopped painting because I wouldn't allow myself to paint until I understood that. And now I totally understand that. Now I'm really painting. It's like an extension of me, of my soul.

At times I've done these massive spells of painting, non-stop, working really, really hard, physically really pushing myself. And then I go, "Ugh." And there's nothing left. The last time I did this, I ended up having cancer. It scares me. Either you are using up too much, and it comes out as too much of you. Or your subconscious is aware that time is running out so it pushes the inside of you to get out. Or maybe that stuff coming out *is* the cancer. Maybe that stuff is the brutality of life that exists inside you. Maybe all the paintings I did in 2019 and 2020, two years before, if I hadn't done them, I might have died. Do you see what I mean?

CJM I do.

TE We don't know, do we? But what I do know is it's a different energy for me now. It's not, Oh, should I paint today? When I stopped everything else, and just painted, I realized that it was like the Sufis in the 13th century. They worked out how to split the atom, and then they all were sworn to secrecy because they knew it was too lethal, too dangerous, it could destroy the world. I would say painting is like this. It's like you understand you've got this energy, and you've got to crack it open onto the canvas. And you know that you could be starting the next nuclear war. Of course you're not. It's not that intense, but that's what it feels like. That's what I feel like when I'm painting.

CJM Was it scary when you made the decision to show your paintings in the Venice Biennale in 2007?

TE Well, that was a disaster, right?

CJM Who was it a disaster for?

TE Me.

CJM Okay, but in your honest estimation, are those works a disaster?

TE Some of them. Some of them were brilliant. Some of them weren't. I don't know anyone who would use Venice as a stepping stone.

CJM Yes, but that's what people should do. That's ideally what we go to Venice for — to see new work that hasn't been seen before — and then instead we see things that are boring or market-driven or classic.

TE I don't think my show was boring.

CJM It wasn't boring. That's what I'm saying. So, why was it a disaster?

TE When I did Venice, I had a studio with about thirty paintings in it that were insane and wild. I didn't have the confidence to show them, but at the same time, I had a show at Gagosian in the September after Venice, and they didn't encourage me to show those paintings, because they needed them. And I should have just said, "Fuck you. Fuck my show at Gagosian. I'm not doing it. Sorry. She has canceled. Sue me. Do whatever the fuck you want. I've got Venice, and I'm showing those paintings."

Andrea Rose [commissioner for the British Pavilion] was brilliant. She could have selected the best of Tracey Emin. It could have been twenty-five blankets, and some neon, and all the overseas people would go, "Oooh." But I told Andrea, "I can't do that." Also, I didn't think I was going to get Venice. No one wanted me to have it. There was a backlash against me at the time. I found out I had Venice six months before Venice.

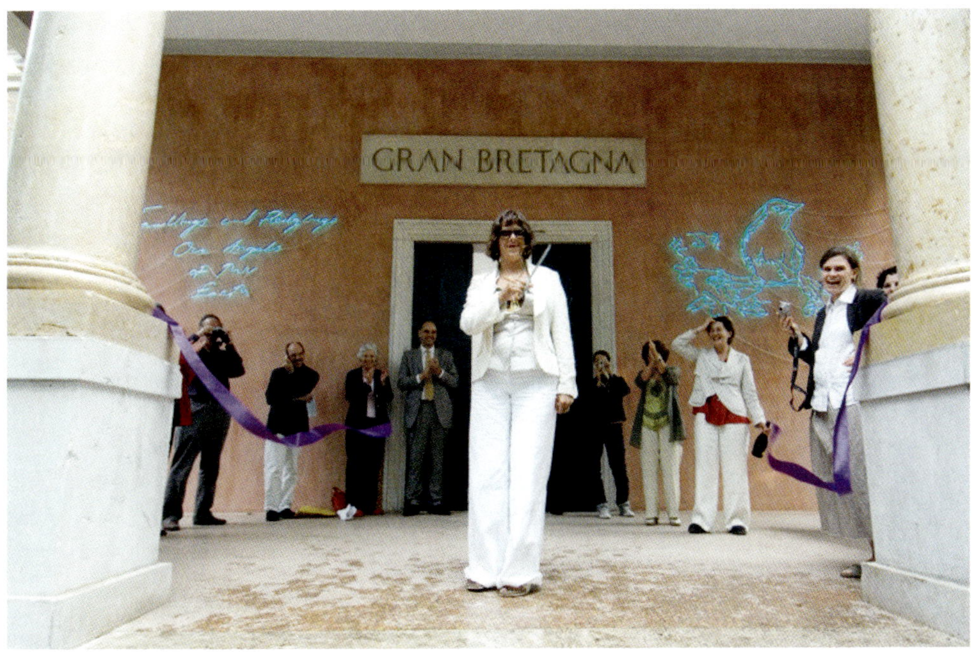

Tracey Emin at the British Pavilion, Venice, 2007

CJM That's not even enough time to get the works shipped there.

TE Right, and I had just written a book called *Strangeland*. And in my book contract I had to go to every fucking town in Britain doing book signings. Whereas now, I would just say, "Sorry, I just got Venice. I'm not doing the book signings. Again, sue me, do whatever you like." This was the biggest moment of my life and my career. It's Venice. And then, of course, being Tracey, I spent all my budget for Venice on restoring the pavilion. The pavilion had holes in it.

CJM It did. It was in horrible shape.

TE I spent nearly all my budget on renovating it—from the floorboards to taking all the paint off the marble to putting the windows back in. And not one person thanked me for that. Really, what I should have done was just shown all the paintings that were in my studio. But I didn't. I showed sculptures, which were actually quite interesting, if you were interested in sacred geometry. But they were in wood, painted with bits of gesso, not bronze, because I didn't have time to make them out of bronze. That show was what I was working on then and some older pieces for context, which I always include when I hang a show. But it was about being sexually abused as a teenager, about this buildup of being a woman, and that doesn't really go down too well in Venice, on the whole. Although, lo and behold, twenty years later, they have a whole Venice about these kinds of issues. But not in my year. The fact that I'm half-Turkish, Cypriot—that was not considered in terms of my Venice presentation.

But the good thing was Andrea Rose was really supportive and loved my paintings, especially my very innocent, very free paintings. I showed them at Gagosian. Sold all of them, like you do. And I carried on painting and painting until I got better and better and better and understood what I was doing. And then one day I walked to the studio, got rid of all the fabric, got rid of all the people, got rid of everything, and just painted. It was the best thing I ever did.

CJM Today, physically, can you paint on your own? Can you still pick up a canvas?

TE Well, sometimes other people move them. But sometimes, all on my own, with all my strength from life, I'll move a canvas. But usually, because my studio in Margate is so big now, I can have twenty paintings on the go, and just keep moving and moving. When Harry [Weller, Creative Director of Emin's studio] comes down, he moves the finished ones to the back of the stack of paintings. Other times I'll paint over another painting that has no legs. I like the power in making those decisions.

I don't drink anymore, but before, I would be on my own till 4:00 or 5:00 in the morning, get really drunk, fall asleep, get up again, paint at 7:00. And I'd go, "Oh, no." Because I'd painted over a really good painting. One of the best paintings I've ever done is underneath a black painting that says, "I wanted to fuck you so much, I couldn't paint anymore." I've still got a picture of it. It was shocking how good it was, this painting. Even I couldn't believe I'd done it. And now it's gone, because I painted over it.

CJM The way you paint is very physical, very muscular.

TE Yes, when I was ill after the chemo, I couldn't paint for a year. Then when I started painting, I couldn't bend, or sweep, or anything. Then one night, I just said to Harry, "I feel like I've never had cancer." It's like I never had my bladder cut out. It's like I'm twenty-five, and I'm just moving gracefully across the canvas. It's a fantastic feeling, like absolute freedom. I paint a big red stroke, and it all floods down, and then I get a sponge and rub it, and it goes all gray and dark. Then I'll add white over there. And then, *foom*, I can see a person in it. I never know what I'm going to paint, ever.

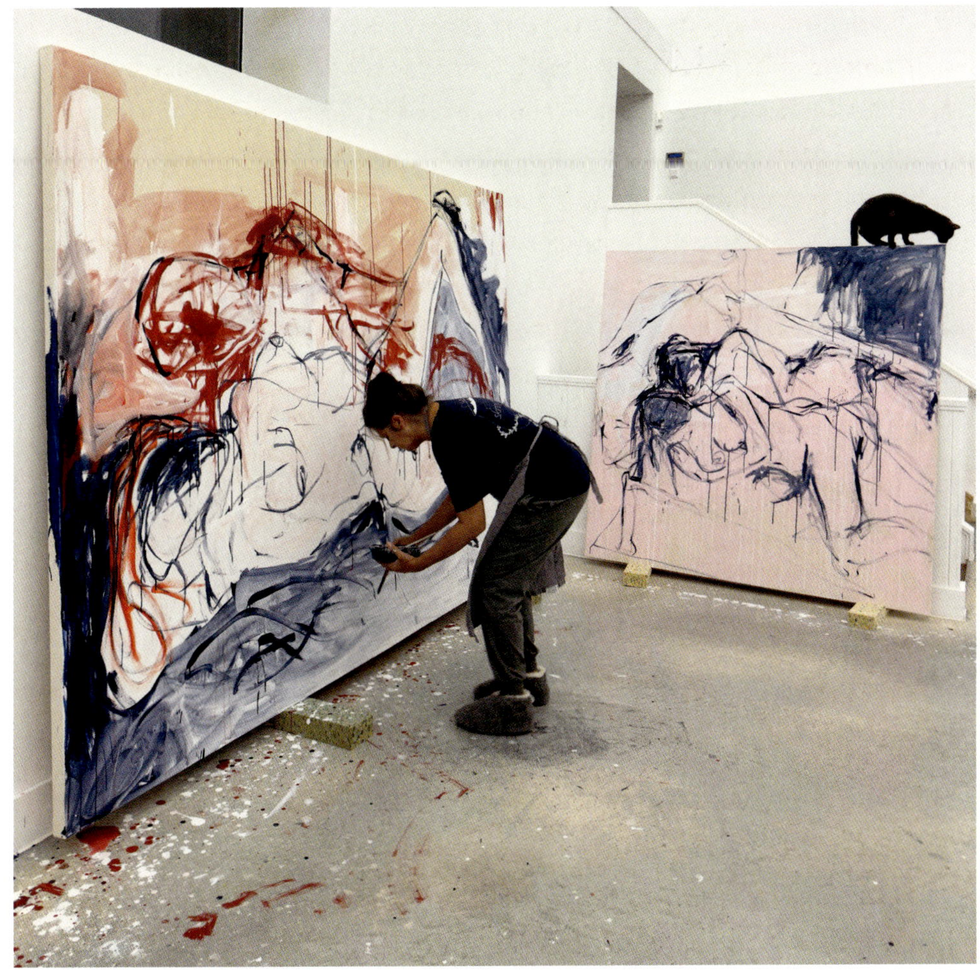

Tracey Emin, Margate, 2024

CJM So the drawings don't feed into the paintings?

TE My little drawings are finished drawings in themselves. My sketchbook's like a diary. When my mum died in 2016, I wanted to change my life. So, I thought, I am never, ever, ever, going to scale up a drawing from the sketchbook. I have to do a completely different drawing. It can't be the same drawing.

CJM Why not?

TE Because it's not real. My mark-making intuitively takes some kind of shape. I do a drawing, a big drawing, and then I think, I'll put turquoise blues across it. And then I'll suddenly go, Oh my God, that drawing's awful. And I'll paint it all out white or pink or something. Then I add a ton of Payne's gray. It's my main drawing color. If it's thick, it's very blue, and if it's thin, it's very gray. And you can just use it as is or dilute it. But, red, I have tons of reds, maybe eight different reds on the go that are mixed up. And when I use them, a painting can start to vibrate, do stuff, tell me stuff.

So it's the color, the shapes, the images, the emotion, the drips, the spontaneity, and the lack of fear, as well. Most of the time you are fearful, and then there's this moment when you're not at all, and something really insane happens. Here's an example. On a really big canvas, I drew this big red mark. And then I thought, Ooh, legs wide open. I drew this almost schoolboy vagina. Then this body, and then this head. And then I painted it out, and then I painted it back in. And then I sat with it in my studio for ages. And I thought, It's fucking brilliant, because I've never seen anything like it before in my life. It was so shocking.

And this sounds pathetic, but I do this thing in my head where after I finish a painting, I imagine I'm at Art Basel, and I come across this painting. Do I stand here and look at it? Do I walk past? I see someone and they ask, "Seen anything you like?" And they go, "No, but there's this really weird painting of these legs wide open and this really badly drawn vagina. Have you seen it?" I hear what other people say in my head. Their shock. It's always at a fucking art fair. It's never in a museum, it's never in a gallery. I put my painting in this really gross environment, with hundreds of other artworks, and mentally I see how it survives, how it battles for its little corner. So it's like when I was young, I got it right, imagining my work in the National Gallery, and now I do this, which is a bit pathetic. But it's the truth. I do draw a line at auction houses though. I won't bid on my own work, and I tell my galleries not to.

CJM Do you ever want to bid on them, because you miss them?

TE I don't want anyone bidding on my work as an investment for the future or to save my integrity. I want them to really want it. The painting is real. It has energy. When someone puts it in their home, it's all my energy pulsing there, changing their walls, changing their atmosphere. I did bid on the *Exorcism* on my own. But why should I have to buy my own work back? It is my work. No one can take my work away from me. It's still mine.

CJM You're painting primarily at Margate now. I understand it to be a very large space. Is that going to change the scale of your work?

TE I've been painting there since 2022, and before, even in a little studio, I painted quite big. But in that studio, I can work on four big paintings. In Margate, I can work on eighteen paintings that are double the size.

CJM Do you work on multiple paintings at one time?

TE Yes. The more I have, the more I can jump around, throw my paint everywhere, and enjoy it. If I just work on one, I have to sit around waiting for the paint to dry. I also have some paintings that I don't touch for five or seven years, and then I pull them out again.

CJM What's the longest you've worked on one painting?

TE I think one took me ten years, from beginning to the end. But I've got one canvas, a small one, that I started in 2004, and it's not finished yet. I used to date my paintings with the beginning and the end, but now we just date them when they're finished, and then write a note about when it started, explaining it. Some of my paintings start off with text on them. Then when the text is gone, I even forget there was text. If they were X-rayed, you would see all these layers. But the paint looks so thin and fresh, you don't know there are layers.

CJM Are you sanding between the layers? Is that how the paint seems so thin?

TE No, it's thin paint. Some are just two layers, but some of them, if you look from the side, you can see many layers of paint. I use very, very thin paint. I've never needed to use great big, thick, macho globules of paint. I always had to make something that comes from the deepest part of my soul, and in the end, this was going to be with painting. I realize now that for years and years I had to build this foundation of ideas — writing, embroidery, films, photography, everything — this whole catalogue, this mountain for me to stick my flagpole on top of and say, "This is where I am. This is who I am." That's what I'm doing now with the painting. The paintings are the flag, and all the other things are the ground that carried me here.

EXHIBITION CHECKLIST

PAINTINGS

1   *Hurricane* 2007
Acrylic on canvas
72 × 72 in. (183 × 183 cm)
FAMM Museum, Mougins, France /
The Levett Collection

2   *Pelvis High* 2007
Acrylic, oil pastel, and pencil on canvas
71⅞ × 71⅞ in. (182.5 × 182.5 cm)
Private collection

3   *A rose* 2007
Acrylic on canvas
72 × 72 in. (183 × 183 cm)
Private collection

4   *Black Cat* 2008
Acrylic on canvas
72 × 59⅞ in. (183 × 152 cm)
Private collection

5   *I said No* 2005–15
Acrylic on canvas
72 × 72 in. (182.9 × 182.9 cm)
Collection of Gianfranco D'Amato

6   *Sometimes There is No Reason* 2018
Acrylic on canvas
48 × 48¼ in. (122 × 122.5 cm)
Private collection

7   *And So It Felt Like This* 2018
Acrylic on canvas
72⅝ × 48½ in. (184.4 × 123.2 cm)
Private collection

8   *I never Asked to Fall in Love –
You made me Feel like This* 2018
Acrylic on canvas
72 × 84⅝ in. (182.8 × 214.8 cm)
Private collection

9   *I wanted you to Fuck The inside
of my mind* 2018
Acrylic on canvas
71⅝ × 59⅞ in. (182 × 152 cm)
Private collection

10   *You Held my Face* 2018
Acrylic on canvas
59⅞ × 72⅛ in. (152.1 × 183.1 cm)
Private collection

11   *Ghost of you* 2018
Acrylic on canvas
60⅛ × 59⅞ in. (152.6 × 152 cm)
Forman Family Collection

12   *I said I would say goodbye* 2019
Acrylic on canvas
71¾ × 59⅞ in. (182.1 × 152.2 cm)
Private collection

13   *You kept it coming* 2019
Acrylic on canvas
60 × 60 in. (152.3 × 152.3 cm)
Private collection

14   *From The Mountain to The Lake*
2022
Acrylic on canvas
71⅝ × 84¼ in. (182 × 214 cm)
Courtesy the artist

15   *Dreaming of Another World*
2022
Acrylic on canvas
36 × 48⅛ in. (91.5 × 122.1 cm)
Collection of Rob Hayes

16   *I wanted to be clean* 2023
Acrylic on canvas
71¾ × 47¼ in. (182.2 × 120 cm)
Collection Frederic Court

17   *And It was Love* 2023
Acrylic on canvas
80 7/8 × 110 in. (205.5 × 279.5 cm)
Courtesy the artist

18   *Don't Ask me to be like you* 2024
Acrylic on canvas
71 3/4 × 47 3/8 in. (182.1 × 120.3 cm)
Private collection

19   *I Followed you to the end* 2024
Acrylic on canvas
71 3/4 × 47 1/4 in. (182.2 × 120.1 cm)
Yale Center for British Art, gift of the
George Economou Collection

SCULPTURE

20   *Without conscience* 2014
Bronze, edition of 6
12 × 16 × 32 in. (30.5 × 40.6 × 81.3 cm)
Courtesy the artist

21   *Every part of me feels you* 2014
Bronze, edition of 6
11 × 36 × 17 in. (27.9 × 91.4 × 43.2 cm)
Courtesy the artist

22   *Landscape* 2016
Bronze, edition of 6, with 2 APs
9 1/2 × 24 3/4 × 15 in. (24 × 63 × 38 cm)
Courtesy the artist

DRAWINGS

23   *My heart my soul my body —
Every — Thing shook* 2021
India ink on lithograph
30 3/4 × 37 1/4 in. (78 × 94.5 cm)

24   *Angels Every where All the time* 2021
India ink on lithograph
30 7/8 × 36 3/8 in. (78.3 × 92.5 cm)

25   *Some Things make No difference*
2022
India ink on lithograph
30 3/4 × 37 1/4 in. (78 × 94.5 cm)

26   *You were supposed to have
loved me* 2023
India ink on lithograph
30 3/4 × 37 1/4 in. (78 × 94.5 cm)

27   *In The darkest days* 2023
India ink on lithograph
30 3/4 × 37 5/8 in. (78 × 95.6 cm)

28   *US — All of Us* 2024
Acrylic on paper
4 1/8 × 5 7/8 in. (10.6 × 14.8 cm)

29   *More Of Us* 2024
Acrylic on paper
4 1/8 × 5 7/8 in. (10.6 × 14.8 cm)

30   *MAGIC Carpet Again* 2024
Acrylic on paper
4 1/8 × 5 7/8 in. (10.6 × 14.8 cm)

31   *CAT* 2024
Acrylic on paper
4 1/8 × 5 7/8 in. (10.6 × 14.8 cm)

32   *I Fly* 2024
Acrylic on paper
4 1/8 × 5 7/8 in. (10.6 × 14.8 cm)

33   *Tea Ceremony* 2024
Acrylic on paper
4 1/8 × 5 7/8 in. (10.6 × 14.8 cm)

34   *Ancient Love* 2024
Acrylic on paper
4 1/8 × 5 7/8 in. (10.6 × 14.8 cm)

35   *I Saw you looking at me* 2024
Acrylic on paper
5 7/8 × 4 1/8 in. (14.8 × 10.6 cm)

*All drawings in exhibition
from the Tracey Emin Archive*

NEON

*I Loved You Until The Morning
2025**
Neon
6 ft. 6 in. × 14 ft. (198.2 × 426.7 cm)
Collection of the artist

** fabricated after publication*

ACKNOWLEDGMENTS

*The following people and institutions have made essential contributions
to this exhibition and catalogue, for which we are deeply grateful.*

ARTIST/STUDIO

Tracey Emin

Harry Weller

BENEFACTORS

George Economou Collection

Arthur W. Zeckendorf

ARTIST'S GALLERIES

White Cube

  Cecily Bates

  Emily Ehrman

  Susanna Greeves

  Jay Jopling

  Honey Luard

  Susan May

  Courtney Willis Blair

Xavier Hufkens

  Myrna D'Ambrosio

  Xavier Hufkens

  Herbert van Litsenburg

  Grace Lockwood

Galleria Lorcan O'Neill Roma

  Laura Chiari

  Lorcan O'Neill

LENDERS

Frederic Court

Gianfranco D'Amato

Tracey Emin

FAMM Museum, Mougins, France/
  The Levett Collection

Forman Family Collection

Rob Hayes

Private collections

RESEARCH SUPPORT

Kraig Binkowski

Brooke Krancer

Rachel Stratton

Daniel Zhang

FABRICATION

Jeff Friedman

PHOTOGRAPHY CREDITS

Every effort has been made to credit the photographers and sources. If there are any errors or omissions, please contact the Yale Center for British Art so that corrections can be made in any subsequent edition.

All works by Tracey Emin © 2025 Tracey Emin / DACS, London / Artists Rights Society (ARS), New York. All rights reserved. Unless otherwise indicated below, all images are courtesy Tracey Emin Studio.

© ADAGP, Paris, photo Giusti Claudio: 43 (pl. 1)

Courtesy the artist and Xavier Hufkens, photo HV-Studio: 52–53 (pl. 8), 55 (pl. 10), 57 (pl. 12), 59 (pl. 13)

© British Council, photo Prudence Cuming Associates Ltd.: 29 (fig. 7), 117

Courtesy Collection Majudia, photo © David Parry/Royal Academy of Arts: 109

Courtesy Tracey Emin © Laurence King Publishing, photo David Dawson: 15 (fig. 1)

Courtesy Gagosian Gallery Los Angeles, photo Douglas M. Parker Studio: 32 (fig. 9), 45 (pl. 3)

Courtesy Galleria Lorcan O'Neil, photo Mike Bruce: 49 (pl. 5)

Photo Ollie Harrop: 36 (fig. 11), 63 (pl. 16), 66 (pl. 18), 67 (pl. 19), 106

Photo HV-Studio: 80 (figs. 5, 6)

Courtesy Lehmann Maupin, photo Elisabeth Bernstein: 73 (pl. 22)

© Murdo Photo: 24 (fig. 5)

Photo Prudence Cuming Associates Ltd.: 10, 54 (pl. 9), 56 (pl. 11), 60 (pl. 14), 61 (pl. 15), 64–65 (pl. 17), 76 (figs. 1, 2), 91–105 (pls. 23–35), 113; scan by Happy Retouching: 84 (fig. 10)

Courtesy The Saatchi Gallery, London, photo Prudence Cuming Associates Ltd.: 26 (fig. 6)

Photo Harry Weller: 35 (fig. 10), 119

Courtesy White Cube: photo Theo Christelis: 50 (pl. 6), 51 (pl. 7); photo Antonia Reeve: 18 (figs. 2A & B); photo Todd-White Art Photography: 44 (pl. 2), 47 (pl. 4); photo Ben Westobv: 69 (pl. 20), 71 (pl. 21); photo Stephen White: 22 (figs. 4A & B), 30 (fig. 8)

Published in conjunction with the exhibition *Tracey Emin: I Loved You Until The Morning,* organized by Martina Droth, Deputy Director and Chief Curator, Yale Center for British Art, New Haven, Connecticut, March 29 – August 10, 2025

The exhibition is generously supported by Arthur W. Zeckendorf.

Produced by the Department of Publications
Yale Center for British Art
Don McMahon, Head of Publications
Julie Fry, Head of Design

Design and production by Julie Fry
Edited by Jennifer Liese
Proofread by A. F. Dunlap Smith
Printed and bound by Graphius, Ghent

Typeset in Area and Miller
Printed on GardaPat Bianka

Published by the Yale Center for British Art
britishart.yale.edu

ISBN: 978-0-300-27972-6
Library of Congress Control Number: 2024948113

Distributed by Yale University Press
New Haven and London
yalebooks.com
yalebooks.co.uk

Jacket illustrations
Front: *From The Mountain to The Lake,* 2022 (detail of plate 14)
Back: *I Followed you to the end,* 2024 (plate 19)

Cover and half-title page
Sketch for fabrication of *I Loved You Until The Morning,* 2025

Printed and bound in Belgium